The incalculable impa  ntelligence, and spiritual ap nizes the impact of not al nces. Instead, Bishop Joseph Walker's new book, *Restored at the Root*, points to the often invisible attacks that threaten our wholeness. Furthermore, it offers therapy in a book! If you've ever felt overwhelmed but couldn't fully identify the root causes, this will truly help! It is a must-read in the turbulence of our times!

—T. D. JAKES SR.
SENIOR PASTOR, THE POTTER'S HOUSE OF DALLAS

Restored at the Root is a must-read for anyone looking to reboot emotionally, spiritually, and mentally. Bishop Walker will help you find restoration in the area of your life where you need it the most. Of all his books, this is the most timely and timeless. It will bless you beyond measure!

—DEVON FRANKLIN
NEW YORK TIMES BEST-SELLING AUTHOR
HOLLYWOOD PRODUCER

Bishop Joseph Walker has led his church to become a congregation with a global impact. At the heart of his ministry is his commitment to his congregants' fulfilling their callings in Christ. That's why this book is so important. Bishop Walker addresses the root causes of our frustrations. Moreover, he gives us effective ways to deal with them. Read this book.

—MIKE GLENN
SENIOR PASTOR, BRENTWOOD BAPTIST CHURCH

This powerful book by my presiding bishop gets to the root of the spiritual, emotional, and social struggles of today. In Luke 11:21–22 Jesus said, "When a strong man, fully armed [with gifts, talent, money, education, etc.], guards his own palace, his goods are in peace. But when a stronger than he comes upon him and overcomes him, he takes from him all his armor [all the natural things] in which he trusted." You need a stronger One than you. The power of God will be your victory. This is the book you have been waiting for. *Restored at the Root* helps you deal with you. Read, enjoy, and above all learn about you.

—Bishop Paul S. Morton
Founder, Full Gospel Baptist Church Fellowship
Pastor, Changing a Generation Full Gospel Baptist
Church

RESTORED
AT THE
ROOT

RESTORED
AT THE
ROOT

JOSEPH W. WALKER III, DMin

CHARISMA
HOUSE

Scripture quotations marked NLT are from the Holy Bible, New Living Translation, copyright © 1996, 2004, 2007. Used by permission of Tyndale House Publishers, Inc., Wheaton, IL 60189. All rights reserved.

Visit the author's website at www.josephwalker3.org and RestoredAtTheRoot.com.

Library of Congress Cataloging-in-Publication Data:
An application to register this book for cataloging has been submitted to the Library of Congress.
International Standard Book Number: 978-1-62999-668-4
E-book ISBN: 978-1-62999-669-1

19 20 21 22 23 — 987654321
Printed in the United States of America

Contents

Introduction

WITH THE BOOKS I have written, before putting pen to paper, I was prayerfully sensitive to the audience to which I was writing. The same is true of this work. When I first began pondering the message God had given me for this book, I was poised to address those currently in the crosshairs of the enemy, as well as those in the trenches ministering to and interceding for people under spiritual attack. These groups of people would relate to and benefit most from this work. However, after I began writing, it did not take long for me to self-identify with both groups. I needed to hear these words too!

I have a personal connection with this subject because I had to go through it firsthand in order to present this work with integrity. Self-realization has brought me to a place of incredible transparency. I share this because I understand the importance and power of speaking one's truth. Courage, honesty, and vulnerability are all necessary to the process of being restored at the root. Struggle is universal, and all of us have underlying struggles that must be confronted. Because I have gone through and continue to go through seasons of spiritual attack, I want you to know you are not alone. We are all on this journey together, seeking to be heard and restored.

This fight is not easy. The journey can be exhausting. But we cannot faint in this process. At all costs we must dig deep and pull to the surface the good, bad, and ugly in order to set in motion the deliverance we so desperately need.

Have you ever asked yourself, "Why do I do what I do? What's wrong with me?" I know I have. I've often tried to stop doing things that were not spiritually healthy. However, I felt like Paul in Romans 7:18, where he said, "For I know that good itself does not dwell in me, that is, in my sinful nature. For I have the desire to do what is good, but I cannot carry it out" (NIV).

I'm convinced that many Christians spend the majority of their lives living beneath God's intent. We wrestle with so many issues that prevent us from experiencing our full potential, never realizing what is at the root of our struggle. And if we do recognize the root issue, we don't know what to do about it. Spiritual attacks are demonic assaults on the mind, body, or spirit. They are coordinated efforts "to oppress a believer, abort promises, shipwreck faith, and stall out destiny."[1] These attacks threaten God's will for your life and can manifest in a variety of ways, including in the form of sexual, drug, or alcohol addictions; depression; anxiety; or low self-worth. The pressure from an attack can create unbearable frustration, hopelessness, and loss of focus, making you unable to function in the purposes of God.

The goal of the attack is to systematically destroy your

character, your family, your destiny, and your life. The devil's intent is to infiltrate your spirit and leave you in a reprobate state to render you incapable of making a righteous decision. The enemy can be relentless, which has led some to simply accept their struggles and believe they are impossible to overcome. But nothing could be further from the truth. Jesus won the victory over Satan on the cross—"having disarmed principalities and powers, He made a public spectacle of them, triumphing over them in it" (Col. 2:15).

My prayer is that this book will help you understand not only the "what" of the attacks upon your life but also the "why." Being restored at the root is about recognizing Satan's plot against you, dismantling it, and refusing to participate in your own demise. This book is about going through the process of reclaiming the life God intended for you.

We live in a world that is content with diagnosing behavior rather than exploring the underlying issues that give rise to it. This has caused us to respond to people and to our personal struggles in ways that may not be beneficial. Our churches are filled with disillusioned and discouraged members because so many have not been able to find true deliverance and healing. We have developed the skill of functioning in dysfunction and masking our mess so we can do what we are assigned to do. I believe for us to live out the gospel and our God-given assignments, we must shift from focusing on "doing" to actually "being."

If we are serious about being who God has called us to be, we must examine the source of our struggles. Every action has a cause. Something deeper may be influencing what we see on the surface. We must be willing to go to the root and unravel layers of hidden issues that are contributing to the chaos in our lives. When our roots are restored, we can experience true freedom in Christ.

One day while visiting my hometown of Shreveport, Louisiana, I saw something in nature that spoke to me spiritually. There was a huge tree with branches that had no leaves or fruit. This struck me as odd because I remembered seeing similar trees when I was growing up that were full of fruit at that exact time of year. I was baffled by the fact that the tree had grown so tall yet had not produced any fruit. My friend, who is very familiar with plants and nature, explained to me that something was wrong at the root of the tree. Although it did not prevent the tree from growing taller and its branches from extending, it did prevent it from producing fruit. This tree had everything but the thing that gave it purpose: fruit!

There are people who have positions and titles, yet their lives produce no fruit. They have grown taller in society and gained more visibility, yet they have not realized their maximum potential because of root issues. When there is a problem at the root, it affects the fruit. Jesus said in John 15:8, "Herein is my Father glorified, that ye bear much fruit; so shall ye be my disciples" (KJV). In my hometown I noticed this massive tree that was occupying space yet was producing nothing. It is not the will of God that we occupy space in the earth and our lives yield no fruit. If you want to produce to the glory of God, you must be willing to be restored at the root. Whatever happens to the tree above ground is in direct relationship with what happens beneath the ground.

For years I've seen Christians struggle privately, attempting to maintain a public image. We have become expert doers while simultaneously sacrificing our integrity. This facade has normalized our dysfunction, causing us to live the paradox of public acclaim and private turmoil. This state of affairs has contributed to the increased suicide rate within the church. Leaders and laity alike have contemplated things they never imagined they would, all because their private struggles were threatening their public persona.

We have seen so many in the kingdom succumb to their private struggles through public exposure, humiliation, and shame. Many people stretch themselves with the demands of work and ministry. I've seen great people bury themselves in their careers in an effort to appear successful. I've seen people volunteer in every ministry to appear busy for God when in fact they were using these moments to mask deeper struggles they were not ready to confront. My wife often tells of a conversation she had with one of her mentors. He had a distinguished career yet found himself incredibly unfulfilled at an old age. His words of wisdom to her were invaluable. Despite all his accomplishments, he had lost his marriage. His children didn't know him as they should. He said to her, "Perhaps if I had written one less paper, taken one less trip, or given one less lecture, things might not have turned out the way they did." Every day you wake up, you should seek God's direction concerning your assignments. If you aren't careful, you will end up getting straight As publicly and Fs privately.

Countless people have sacrificed their families on the altar of ministry because of their need to feel validated.

While doing ministry, they were unable to "be" ministry in their personal lives. I've spoken to so many people, laity and leaders alike, who were in conflict because the demand to continue to produce didn't provide space for them to work through many of their private struggles. I believe all of us, regardless of our professions, get consumed with the expectations of people and often neglect what we need for inner healing to take place. Living in unresolved conflict is neither helpful nor productive. If true healing is to occur, we must be willing to face our issues. I've said on numerous occasions that you cannot fix what you are not ready to face. This book is about helping you break the addiction, cancel the generational curse, stop the cycle of dysfunction, and end the masquerade.

We live in an image-focused society. Social media has given people a platform to create images of themselves that insulate them and others from their true reality. The unfortunate consequence of what we are seeing in culture is slowly permeating the pews. Too many churches are more focused on their brand than the blood of Jesus. Congregants are being caught in the vortex of pretentiousness, which makes it increasingly more difficult to accept the truth about their current situation and take the necessary steps toward healing. False image breeds denial, which attracts a multitude of demonic spirits in our lives. The devil is drawn to lies and deceit, and when we are dismissive of truth, we invite attack. John 8:44 reminds us that Satan is the father of lies. His first attack on Adam and Eve was to be dismissive of God's truth and create a false image that downplayed the consequences of rebellion. This is a tactic he still uses today.

Many people who experience spiritual attack are not aware that Satan desires to drag them into deception. Once deception has taken root, denial sets in, which ultimately leads to destruction. John 10:10 says, "The thief does not come except to steal, and to kill, and to destroy. I have come that they may have life, and that they may have it more abundantly." Jesus has come to deliver us to the quality of life God desired for us in the beginning. Christ's coming was God's act of restoration to those who had been deceived by the enemy.

A BLUEPRINT FOR FREEDOM

The good news is that whatever entrapments we find ourselves in, God has given us a blueprint in His Word for how to break free. Deliverance is progressive. It is a process that requires a desire to pursue truth. I liken it to a series of concentric circles. Perception is the outer realm, and as you work inward, the next realm is your image. As you progress

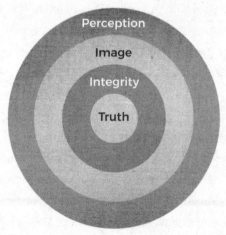

further inward, you come to integrity before arriving at the core, which is the truth.

Perception is based on who people think we are. It's very easy to create a perception of yourself that is inconsistent with who you really are. One lie, one erroneous post on social media, or an unrelenting desire not to live in reality will do the trick.

Sadly so many people have remained in the realm of perception, and doing so has caused them to move seamlessly into the next realm of creating an image to support it. Once people believe the lie about you, you must constantly present an image to mask it. If a person is perceived as having a certain amount of money, that individual may go into debt to convince people that their perception is not wrong. Conversely, if it is erroneously perceived that someone has high character, that person may create an image of trustworthiness only to gain access and cause harm.

The next realm is integrity. This is when you are willing to have the tough conversation about where you are in your life. It is the point in life the prodigal son experienced in the pigpen when he "came to himself." I've heard many people in church refer to this realm as "sick and tired of being sick and tired." Integrity is not concerned with perception or image. It raises questions nobody else has. Perception is who people think you are, but integrity is who you really are. This is where the real work takes place before you enter the final realm of truth. Once you arrive at truth, you are like Adam and Eve were in the garden. You are "naked and not ashamed." Truth is the place of complete deliverance and healing. Truth is the place where you are more aligned with God than ever before.

Jesus declared in John 8:32, "You shall know the truth, and the truth shall make you free." This book is about living in the truth at the root of our lives. It's about getting you beyond the realms of perception and image and pushing you into integrity and truth. Those who are willing to embark upon this journey are courageous. It takes a strong level of commitment to address issues at the root of our lives. This journey could lead you to places in your childhood. It could lead you to moments you had suppressed or even forgotten. It can cause you to confront the memory of very traumatic seasons in your past.

Your struggle had a genesis. Some event spawned a series of other events that manifested in your struggles today. This book is about discovering the intersectionality of all your life experiences and helping you work through the impact each has had on you. You don't have to pretend another day. You don't have to worry about perception as you go through this process. All you need is a desire to be truthful about the things that have happened and to live in truth from this day forward.

Jesus' encounter in Mark 5 with a man with an unclean spirit reveals to us the work it takes for healing and deliverance to truly manifest in our lives, and it will serve as the backdrop for this book. I've written this book to be a guide that leads you through the process of self-discovery. Each chapter will help you understand how you arrived in your struggle and will give you a practical strategy to overcome it. I've placed important questions at the end of each chapter called "Root Work" that you can use to assess where you are in the process and discover what is needed to move closer to a place of healing. I encourage you to go through this process of root work prayerfully and carefully.

Satan specializes in hiding behind perception and image, but if you desire to be healed and delivered from the pain of your past and the peril of your present situation so you can live in the light of truth, victory is available to you through Jesus Christ. But this is not a sprint; it is a marathon. You may have a few setbacks along the way. Get back up and start again. This process is too important for you not to complete. Your destiny is at stake. What you do now will impact generations to come. If you are willing to put in the work, addressing not only the symptoms but also the root causes, you will experience restoration in every area of your life.

My prayer is that as you read this, you will draw strength and strategy to aid you in your fight against the enemy. I want you to remember you are victorious in Christ and possess the power to overcome whatever is trying to overtake you. May you realize that you are not your labels, neither can you be reduced down to someone else's definition of you. God calls you to life and liberty! Your current situation is not your final destination. Let the Spirit of our Redeemer guide you as you investigate the root causes of your greatest struggles. Let's go all in and be restored at the root!

CHAPTER 1

Mitigation:
You Can't Fix It if You Don't Face It

IN THE FIFTH chapter of the Gospel of Mark, Jesus encountered a man in the country of the Gadarenes who had an unclean spirit. The spirit had such complete control over the man that it caused him to cut himself and cry out from his residence among the tombs. The story is further complicated by the fact that no one in the community was able to tame him, and in a futile attempt to do so, they put him in chains.

The spirit was so violent, the man constantly broke the shackles. But no matter how many chains he broke, he could never break free of the internal bondage, the spiritual enslavement this spirit imposed on his life. Have you ever identified something you felt was causing your turmoil, mastered it, and still found yourself feeling defeated? I have! It is exhausting and discouraging. What we learn from the man is that chains are but a fruit—a seed-bearing manifestation but not the source of the bondage. To truly break free, we must get down to the root.

When the man saw Jesus afar off, he ran and worshipped Him. The spirit tormenting the man then questioned Jesus' presence, having an awareness of His power, and a remarkable thing occurred. The spirit negotiated its exit. Jesus cast the spirit out of the man and sent it into some swine that were feeding nearby. As soon as they encountered the spirit, the pigs ran violently down a hill and drowned.

Prior to the man's deliverance, Jesus asked the unclean spirit a question that had never been asked of it before: "What is your name?" The spirit called itself Legion, meaning many. The word itself was common in the Roman Empire, as it was used to describe the largest single unit in the Roman army. This is no coincidence. The unclean spirit that called itself Legion was unique in that it was militaristic in nature. It was vast, combative, aggressive, and unwaveringly devoted to the interest and increase of its kingdom and commander.

Spiritual attacks are meant to accomplish spiritual oppression. The enemy desires to get the victory over you by forcing you to abandon your mission and purpose in life, overwhelming you to the point you want to withdraw from the fight, and rendering the weapons of your warfare ineffective. All of this is done with the hope of causing you to surrender.

I tell people if Jesus asks you a question, it is not an attempt to discover something He does not know. He is omniscient, so He knows all things. When He asks you a question, He is doing so to reveal something to you. This man who had been overtaken by an unclean spirit experienced healing and deliverance through a series of life-changing events. The word *mitigate* means to reduce the severity, seriousness, or pain. Let's be clear: our goal is not to simply lessen the pain of our torment; it is to remove it completely. What I am suggesting is that this demon had this man in the tombs like a wild man, and he could not be tamed. For him to experience complete deliverance, there had to be a serious and systematic reduction in how the demon tormented the man.

The only way the man could mitigate the torment in his life was to have a divine encounter. Deliverance does not happen apart from Jesus. He is the Deliverer. But it's difficult to hear Jesus when our pain appears greater than His Word. Often our actions must be toned down in phases so we can experience what we've never encountered before.

When we arrive at our story in Mark 5, Jesus had just spoken peace to a storm. He could have chosen to avoid this situation. But His encounter with the man was a lesson for the disciples and for us so we don't neglect the painful, underlying realities that threaten our lives and those around us. Choosing to avoid the deeper issues that plague us is always an option, but avoidance is detrimental to the process of deliverance.

Let's face it: it's easier not to deal with a problem. It's easy to find refuge in the areas of our lives that are not in conflict. It's easy to focus on our strengths and successes rather than deal with our struggles. I've been there. There have been times in my life when I knew I needed to confront an issue, yet the timing was inconvenient. There are always a thousand excuses lingering when we contemplate addressing the deeper issues that plague our lives.

In Mark 5, people had tried to tame the man and were unsuccessful. We can look around at others who have struggled unsuccessfully with issues much like ours and give up before we even get started. Mitigation is hard work. It is not for the faint of heart. This is why so many take the easy route and avoid it. The journey of deliverance is like peeling an onion. Each layer becomes more difficult because each step of the process stimulates a variety of emotions.

Jesus did not avoid the man's issues. Jesus took the time to face the evil that was tormenting the man, and this is crucial. We come face to face with many issues daily, yet we must decide whether we will address or avoid them. Confronting and casting out evil spirits does not happen by way of quick-fix solutions. A level of investment must be made. Christ came to proclaim good news to the poor, freedom for the prisoners and oppressed, and recovery of sight for the blind. But laying hold of the freedom we have through Christ takes work, intentionality, and a resolve to never quit. The Scripture does not tell us how long Jesus stayed with the man, but we know He did not leave him until he was restored.

If you want to be restored, you must be willing to remain in the process with Jesus and not allow your frustrations to pull you away. There will be challenges and disappointments along the way, but you must be committed to your personal healing. The apostle Paul said,

> Who shall separate us from the love of Christ?
> Shall trouble or hardship or persecution or famine
> or nakedness or danger or sword? As it is written:
> "For your sake we face death all day long: we are
> considered as sheep to be slaughtered." No, in all
> these things we are more than conquerors through
> him who loved us. For I am convinced that neither

> death nor life, neither angels nor demons, neither
> the present nor the future, nor any powers, neither
> height nor depth, nor anything else in all creation,
> will be able to separate us from the love of God that
> is in Christ Jesus our Lord.
>
> —ROMANS 8:35–39, NIV

In the same way, our desire for personal and communal freedom must eclipse our preference to ignore the areas of conflict we or others are facing

THE PROCESS OF DISCOVERY

An attorney friend told me that to litigate a case, discovery is an essential part of the process. In the legal field discovery occurs prior to the trial so that each party can obtain evidence from the other party or parties involved. This can include subpoenas, where people are interrogated in an effort to obtain facts. It is not a pleasant experience, but it is necessary to adequately litigate a case. Emotions can run high, and what can be unveiled and revealed can be incredibly unpleasant. There is a discovery process on the journey to freedom.

Once the hidden is revealed, we may find ourselves going down paths that are unfamiliar as we begin to deal with years of issues that have been lying dormant. This is why it can be difficult for many people who have created certain personas to address their root issues. They fear it might shatter what people have come to believe about them. However, if the discovery never takes place, the case will never be resolved. This unpleasant process must take place to make right the wrongs that have occurred in your life. But you are not going through it alone. Just as with litigation the process of discovery will be handled by an expert to ensure the least amount of harm will result. That expert is Jesus! You cannot do this apart from a relationship with Him.

When the root of the issue is uncovered, the revelation will bring you face to face with the demons behind the spiritual attacks. In his novel *The Last Battle*, C. S. Lewis wrote, "People shouldn't call for demons unless they really mean what they say."[1] We can go a step further and say people shouldn't call for demons unless they are equipped to go into a time of warfare with the demons. Demons are not your friends, nor do they play fair. Demons come to destroy you, and if you are not prepared to handle the demons, they will overtake you.

In the Book of Acts we see Paul operating in the gifts of God, casting evil spirits out of people. When others saw what Paul was doing, they attempted to imitate his actions. The Scripture records the following occurrence:

> Now God worked unusual miracles by the hands of Paul, so that even handkerchiefs or aprons were brought from his body to the sick, and the diseases left them and the evil spirits went out of them. Then some of the itinerant Jewish exorcists took it upon themselves to call the name of the Lord Jesus over those who had evil spirits, saying, "We exorcise you by the Jesus whom Paul preaches." Also there were seven sons of Sceva, a Jewish chief priest, who did so. And the evil spirit answered and said, "Jesus I

> know, and Paul I know; but who are you?" Then the
> man in whom the evil spirit was leaped on them,
> overpowered them, and prevailed against them, so
> that they fled out of that house naked and wounded.
> —ACTS 19:11–16

The seven sons of Sceva attempted to duplicate the power they saw evident in the life of the apostle without relationship with the source of the power, who is Jesus. The authority you need to find deliverance comes from Him. God doesn't want you to copy someone else or rely on that person's relationship with God. He wants you to have your own. I often say God doesn't anoint copies; He anoints originals. If you are to confront the demonic spirits at the root of your struggle, you cannot rely on others to be strong for you. You must be grounded in your own faith, believe the Word of God for yourself, and consistently communicate with God through prayer. The depth and genuineness of your relationship with Jesus will be evident during spiritual attacks. You must be able to draw strength from your own personal relationship with Jesus rather than seeking strength by attempting to hijack someone else's faith.

JESUS TRANSFORMS

Deliverance is risky because it cannot occur without an unraveling of your current situation. This is what makes the tormented man's encounter with Jesus so timely and remarkable. The Scripture says when Jesus got out of the boat, He was immediately met by the man from the tombs. The compassion of Jesus made it all but certain that this man would not remain in the situation another day. You cannot be in the presence of Jesus and remain the same. His presence is transformative.

Jesus' mission was clear from the beginning when He publicly read the scroll of Isaiah in the synagogue, stating in Luke 4:18, "The Spirit of the Lord is upon me, because he hath anointed me to preach the gospel to the poor; he hath sent me to heal the brokenhearted, to preach deliverance to the captives, and recovering of sight to the blind, to set at liberty them that are bruised" (KJV). Jesus was sent to the earth to bring transformation to the areas in your life that are riddled with torment because of demonic instigation. Jesus came to establish peace in the places that are chaotic. But peace is often won through struggle.

Obtaining peace—real peace—can be a disruptive process. The Bible assures us that when you are in the presence of Jesus, your life will never be the same. We must be clear: the mission of Jesus is to intervene in situations that are dysfunctional to reestablish the intended functionality of the person, place, or thing; therefore He is drawn to circumstances that might be considered complicated. It is because of our familiarity with labels in society that we find ways to characterize the issues connected with spiritual attacks as normative behavior instead of seeing them as the problems they are and calling on the power and presence of Jesus to transform us. There is nothing normal about anxiety or depression or having suicidal thoughts. There is nothing normal about addiction, whether it be to alcohol, food, or drugs.

The Bible says that when the man saw Jesus afar off, he

cried out. His crying out exposed the duality of his existence. One part of him was controlled by the demon, and another part of him protested the oppression. When the protest part of us gets stronger than the controlled part of us, we cry out for help. Crying out manifests in a variety of ways. The man's cries were audible, but some cries are not. Some people cry out and never make a sound. Their crying has become behavioral. Have you ever seen a young person experience internal turmoil and act out in ways that are viewed as disruptive or confusing? Have you ever cried out in the way you performed your task at work or interacted with people close to you?

We often label people based on their behavior and don't realize that they are crying out for help. The labels we put on people can become lifelong stigmas. When labels are placed upon us, our interaction with society becomes more difficult because people see our labels before they see us. Labels dehumanize us and make it easier for people to marginalize us. We become classified as social misfits by people who don't have the skill set or compassion to deal with us.

This particular man was defined by his condition. He was the man in the tombs. There are countless nameless people in the Bible and in our churches who are classified by their problems. The woman who touched the hem of Jesus' garment was called the woman with the issue of blood. And there were others, such as blind Bartimaeus, the woman at the well, and the lame man at the pool of Bethesda. How many classifications have you heard given to people or had placed on you? How many times have you heard someone referred to as the crackhead, the hoodlum, or the harlot?

In a society bent on labeling and categorizing people, redemption is a strange concept. The people around this man offered only condemning means for handling him. They thought tying him up would solve the problem. But he was already bound spiritually, so their efforts were unsuccessful. Jesus was not interested in dominating him; He was interested in delivering him from what oppressed him.

So often we focus on taming the demonic spirit that causes us torment. Even if it is tamed, it is still with you. When you settle for taming a demonic spirit, you have resigned yourself to believing it is a part of who you are. In other words, you give it permission to stay as long as it is quiet or as long as it does not cause too much disruption. Taming the demon is only a temporary fix because demons are vicious.

We cannot be passive with the demonic. Demons are hateful creatures that have no limit to their desire to wreak havoc on your life. This is why mitigation is only the first step; full deliverance must be our goal. Demons cannot be tamed. They are physically strong and have the ability to break through physical chains, as was the case with the man in Mark 5. He would pull apart chains and break shackles into pieces. The evil spirits that had invaded his life were physically strong, but demons have no power over spiritual strength. This explains why, in several instances when Jesus encountered someone with a demon, the demon asked Jesus, "What have I to do with You, Jesus?" (e.g., Mark 5:7).

Because demons have no spiritual power over the Spirit of God, they want to avoid contact with the Deliverer, Jesus. Demons want to maintain control of their territory, and Jesus' presence threatens a demon's ability to continue to oppress a person's life. The attempt to tame a demon is simply another strategy people use to manage a life filled with spiritual torment. But freedom is possible. You must decide today if you want management or a miracle. The spirit you are dealing with is counting on you to give it a leash instead of an eviction notice. It knows it cannot be tamed, so as long as it is allowed to maintain residence, it can still execute its destructive agenda.

Evil spirits are manipulative. I've seen so many people go through life trying to manage spirits that are determined to destroy their lives. To tame it suggests you have it under control. How many people have you heard say, "I've got it under control"? I've never met a person with a drinking problem who didn't think he had it under control. I've never met a person with a drug addiction or any other struggle that didn't feel she had it under control. As you read this, you are probably reflecting on the things you've declared you had under control. Trying to control an issue that has a demonic spirit at the root doesn't make you a bad person, but you must realize that this is a matter of life and death. Your attempts to manage this demonic spirit are putting everything you hold valuable in jeopardy. It's like playing Russian roulette with your destiny.

There is a story of a beaver that was incredibly skillful at crossing the creek. One day a snake approached the beaver and requested a ride on its back to the other side. The snake attempted to make its case by revealing that it was very ill and would die if it didn't get to the other side. The beaver strongly rejected the request, saying he feared the snake would kill him. The snake persisted, insisting that all it wanted was the beaver's compassion so it could get to the other side. This went on for days until the beaver's emotions got the best of him. He felt it was a manageable situation and took the snake at its word. That next morning the snake mounted the beaver as he cautiously ferried the snake across the creek. When the beaver reached the other side, the snake dismounted the beaver and thanked him for saving his life. Then shortly afterward the snake bit the beaver, injecting its poisonous venom into him.

The beaver was bewildered and felt completely betrayed by the snake. As he lay there dying, the beaver asked the snake why he would bite him after receiving assistance that saved his life. The snake's response was simple yet profound. He said, "Because I'm a snake, and this is my nature." Don't lose sight of the fact that you are dealing with demons. No matter what form they take, they are still demons, and they do what demons do.

I'm sure you've had some personal and painful experiences like in the story of the beaver. I've been the beaver on numerous occasions because I have a big heart. What I have learned is that there is a fundamental difference between helping a person and empowering a demon. You have to be spiritual enough to know the difference. Once a demon attacks a life, it has no intentions of goodwill. That is not in its nature. The war between good and evil is real, and you must never let your guard down where demons are concerned.

DEMONS LOOK FOR EMPTY PLACES

To understand the nature of demons, you must be introduced to the origin of demons. Although the origin of demons is not explicitly discussed in the Bible, the New Testament speaks of the fall and subsequent imprisonment of a group of angels: "And the angels who did not keep their proper domain, but left their own abode, He has reserved in everlasting chains under darkness for the judgment of the great day" (Jude 6).

Research into the biblical text further reveals that the kingdom of darkness was created when approximately one-third of the angelic host followed Satan (then Lucifer) in a "foiled insurrection that subsequently led to their expulsion from heaven."[2] Jesus references the fall of Satan in Luke 10:18 when He says, "I saw Satan fall like lightning from heaven." The fall occurred before God created the world, leaving Satan and his angels free to roam the earth and contaminate it with their wickedness. We see evidence of the fall and its impact on the earth in Genesis 1:2: "The earth was without form, and void; and darkness was on the face of the deep. And the Spirit of God was hovering over the face of the waters." The English translation doesn't adequately convey the meaning captured in the original Hebrew. The Hebrew words *tohuw vabohuw*, meaning without form and void,[3] are better translated "waste and void," the terms used in Young's Literal Translation.

Demons want to come in spaces that are without form and that are void so they can give shape to the spaces. That

13

is why they want to occupy the empty spaces in your life. Demons are on a mission to destroy your life, and they gain access through the empty spaces in your life. When demons enter, they kill, steal, and destroy. (See John 10:10.) Whatever you are trying to tie up and tame is too deadly to accommodate another day.

Proverbs 6:27–28 gives a powerful warning against trying to manage demonic spirits: "Can a man take fire in his bosom, and his clothes not be burned? Can one go upon hot coals, and his feet not be burned?" (KJV). A demonic spirit cannot be managed; it must be cast out. But one thing we must learn from this man with the unclean spirit in Mark 5 is that the demon will not be cast out until there is a crying out.

One of the lamentable realities in many of our churches is that many pastors and ministers don't know how to help people who are crying out, so they put systems in place to tie the individuals up or keep them quiet. They control what ministries they allow them to be a part of. They subject them to certain protocols that determine where they sit and don't sit in church. They ostracize them through systems that overtly alienate people and keep them from enjoying the fruits of healthy Christian community. When people don't know what to do with you, they seek to control and contain you. When no programs are available to help you, the church ties you up. When people have not been trained in spiritual warfare and are unable to take authority over the demons that torment you, they tie you up. Spiritual warfare is not something to be feared; it is something we are meant to master. But the only way to gain mastery in a particular area is to have instruction and exposure.

The Bible is our instruction manual, and it is filled with relevant information regarding spiritual warfare and the forces of darkness that wage war against us. The kingdom of darkness is a literal, spiritual kingdom. Therefore we must be knowledgeable about how the kingdom of darkness operates. Ephesians 6:12 declares, "For we wrestle not against flesh and blood, but against principalities, against powers, against the rulers of the darkness of this world, against spiritual wickedness in high places" (KJV). Let's explore this further.

First, it says that we wrestle against principalities. A principality is a state or territory ruled by a prince. In John 12:31 and again in John 14:30 Jesus referenced Satan as being the "prince of this world" (KJV). This implies there are territories being governed by the enemy. There is something vile and dark that occupies these spaces, but you just can't put your finger on what it is. It is important to understand that this cannot be judged solely on the aesthetic of a place. Nicely paved roads and lush green lawns are not indicators of the absence of demonic rule. Remember, this is spiritual, and it must be discerned spiritually.

Furthermore, principalities are often governed by a feudal type of relationship conditioned on the exchange of land for service or labor. Essentially occupants of these areas offer their services, expertise, gifts, talents, and time as rent for maintaining their dwelling place. Part of what we wrestle against is this level of negotiation and compromise, offering allegiance to and defense of things that are harmful, even shameful, all in the name of self-preservation.

Powers and rulers of the darkness are the next mentioned opponents. Powers have been given authority and permission to act, while rulers of the darkness of this world are whatever exercises supremacy and creates dependence. They both deal in influence.

Lastly, we wrestle against spiritual wickedness in high places. The Hebrew word for *high place* is *bamah*, and it usually refers to a place of worship.[4] Using this definition to interpret Ephesians 6:12, a large part of what we are fighting against is not out there in the world somewhere but right in our churches. We are guilty of persistently violating God's command to love all, while worshipping at the altars of proselytism, profits, pleasure, politics, and people-pleasing. Leaders are busy competing over who will be greatest in the kingdom, while entire congregations function like spiritual lynch mobs who partake in the soul killing of anyone who does not look like them or believe what they believe.

Our knowledge of the kingdom of darkness does not make us subject to it because as children of God we have the power to triumph over the spirit of darkness. Light always drives out darkness, and as the light of God in the world we must exercise our authority over darkness. (I'll talk more about how to do that in later chapters.) Jesus triumphed over death, hell, and the grave, and after His resurrection we were given the same authority to triumph over the forces of spiritual darkness. The only thing holding you back from moving from a place of experiencing demonic activity to deliverance in your personal life, your community, and your church body is the misinformation you have received concerning the power you have over the forces of the enemy. You were not meant to live in torment. Your family was never meant to live in torment. The people faithfully attending church were never meant to live with the constant torment of demonic oppression.

The Bible provides us with instruction so that when we are in the midst of a spiritual attack, we will have the information to begin the discovery process and receive revelation of how to conquer what is trying to conquer us. In His postresurrection conversation with the disciples, Jesus shared with them that one of the signs to follow them as believers would be that in His name they would have the ability to cast out demons. Mark 16:17 says, "And these signs shall follow them that believe; in my name shall they cast out devils; they shall speak with new tongues" (KJV).

Please understand this: if you are dealing with demonic oppression, that doesn't mean you don't have an amazing destiny. In fact it is often a sign that the enemy feels threatened by what God can do through you. The destiny upon your life was never meant to be tied up. What Jesus clearly demonstrates is that this man mattered. He mattered to the kingdom. He mattered to God. It's important for you to know that regardless of your struggle you are significant and God absolutely loves you.

The church must not fail God's people by being more concerned about our protocols than people's pain. If people cannot cry out in the church, where can they? Pastors and leaders must create a culture within our churches that not only welcomes the cries of those who are spiritually oppressed but also provides ministry that contributes to their liberation rather than tying them up again. We must be willing to embrace the cries of not only the laity but also leaders. The church should be the safe space where all cries are welcomed.

Maybe you are reading this and you feel nobody hears your cry. It's important that you know even if no one else picks up on your pain, Jesus does. He hears you. He heard you when you were crying out at your desk and couldn't focus. He heard you when you were in the parking lot and tried to find the strength to get out of the car and start your day. He heard you when you were in your bed and turned your face to the wall with tears in your eyes.

Perhaps you are a leader and you are leading while bleeding. You are crying out while pouring into everyone else. He hears you too. You can be in the lowest place possible, but the good news is that the Lord can still hear your cry. In Psalm 40 David described the depth of his crisis as a horrible pit and miry clay. In the midst of it he found comfort knowing that the Lord heard His cry. I've been in situations where I've wondered whether God heard me because people who were close to me didn't. The reality is that often the people closest to us are the last ones to recognize our pain. I want to encourage you to continue crying. Your crying is not a lack of faith, nor does it diminish your witness as a child of God. Keep crying even if it appears nobody is listening.

As a parent I've learned something about the cry of

children. The connection between a parent and a child is so tight that if my child is in a room of fifty other crying babies, I am easily able to identify my child. I can be in another room, but my child's cry has a way of penetrating walls and awakening me from sleep. My love for my children has given me a heightened sensitivity to their cries. No matter what your struggle, you must remember that God loves you beyond anything you could ever imagine.

Regardless of the names people have given you, in God's eyes you are His child. Even if a million cries are simultaneously being directed toward God, He cares so much about you that He knows the unique nature of your cry. It doesn't matter how faint or forceful your cry is; you can have confidence that He hears you. As 1 John 5:14–15 says, "This is the confidence we have in approaching God: that if we ask anything according to his will, he hears us. And if we know that he hears us—whatever we ask—we know that we have what we asked of him" (NIV).

ROOT WORK

1. Are there issues plaguing your life that you don't even want to think about? If the answer is yes, make a list of the issues you would rather avoid, and in one sentence state why you have refused to face what needs to be fixed.

2. What has been your greatest spiritual attack? What was happening in your life before the attack?

3. Have you ever engaged in the process of discovery while going through a spiritual attack? If so, what did you learn about the demons you were fighting?

4. What have you gleaned from past spiritual attacks that you can use to help others?

5. How can you make your environment a safe space for those around you who are crying out because they are in a state of torment?

CHAPTER 2

Location:
How Did I Get Here?

I HAD AN INTERESTING experience walking through the mall one day. On this visit I had planned to go to a specific store that had only recently opened. There was much excitement around this particular store, and I wanted to be one of the first to shop there. Usually, when I go to the mall, I know exactly where to find the store of my choice, but on this particular day I found myself going in circles. I must admit that I'm one of those individuals who will attempt to locate something for a while before seeking directions. After thirty minutes of going in circles, I decided to locate a map of the mall.

The map was huge and had every store in the mall listed by category. As I looked on with great interest, I realized the store I was looking for was on the other side of the mall. It was not a short walk, so I wanted to figure out the best route to get there. After identifying a red dot on the map that said, "You are here," I found the distance to my destination discouraging and daunting at the same time. I was discouraged because after doing my best to locate my destination, I had to embrace the fact that I was nowhere near where I wanted to be. And the distance felt daunting because I could see clearly where I was—the red dot made it obvious—and I was going to have to take a long walk to get to my desired store.

Perhaps as you are reading this book, you are discouraged because you are trying to figure out how you ended up so far from where you desire to be. You did all you could to arrive at the place you were destined to be. But you are staring at your red dot, and you realize you are not even close to your intended destination. If that describes you, you are not alone. Most people have been there at some point in their lives. I know it can be frustrating when you've done your part and yet you are not where you believe God wants you to be.

This is what happened to the man in Mark 5 who was possessed by the demon that called itself Legion. We really don't know why this man was attacked by this demon. In fact even he may not have known why this happened to him. Maybe that's your question: "Why me? Why now?" Rather than being in community with others, enjoying life, and living to his full potential, the man was living in the graveyard. How did he get there? How did you get there?

Understanding where you are in life begins the process of realizing the devil's tactic, which is to isolate you. When you are experiencing a spiritual attack, Satan wants to pull you away from any support system that could assist in your liberation. The alarming part of Satan's isolation method is that he uses it to convince us we will always be bound, even though "it is for freedom that Christ has set us free" (Gal. 5:1,

NIV). The enemy wants you to believe there are no alternatives for you and that you are destined, at best, just to get by. This manipulation of the mind is what leads people to feel stuck in deplorable situations—stuck in places that drain their energy and choke the life out of their visions and purpose and even stuck with people who bring no real value, safety, or wellness to their lives.

But you don't have to remain in that place of isolation. You have a choice to recognize the freedom you have been given. The devil knows you are free, but he uses mental attacks to convince you that you have to remain bound even when there are no physical restraints. Your adversary's tactics include placing you in structures and systems that are invisible yet maintain visible control over you. When the man encountered Jesus, he was not in chains or shackles because he had broken them off. Yet he remained among the tombs.

This is what happens still today. The door to your prison has been unlocked, yet you haven't experienced freedom because the devil has convinced you that the tomb is your new home. He does this to keep you isolated from people who can lead you to a place of liberation. The devil pushes many people to a place of isolation through hurt so deep it produces shame and disillusionment to the degree that they become convinced no one can understand the level of pain they are experiencing. It is apparent that the man in Mark 5 was not welcome in his community, and this is what restricted his freedom. Folks who can offer you only chains cannot lead the charge in your liberation. Yet the fact that he ran to Jesus may suggest that he was looking for an opportunity to connect.

A few years ago I went through one of the most difficult seasons of my life. My first wife was diagnosed with a rare form of cancer called neuroendocrine pancreatic cancer. I will never forget hearing those words from the surgeon who did her biopsy. That diagnosis paralyzed me and changed both our lives forever. We were told she would have up to five years to live, and we both knew this would be the fight of our lives. From age thirty-five to thirty-seven she fought it like a good soldier of Jesus Christ. She was determined to remain in community and regularly attend church services, even when she was not feeling well. After two years of chemotherapy and clinical trials she passed away. Here is where the attack got very real. That Sunday morning when she passed, I was so overtaken with grief I pulled away from everybody and everything. I think that is a natural part of the grieving process; however, I allowed myself to stay in that place too long. I didn't want to be around people, nor did I want to be connected to anything. For months I would preach and then go home and lie in the dark. I was in isolation. I didn't realize what I know now. I was under spiritual attack.

When you are in isolation, you begin to contemplate things you never would have imagined you would consider. This can be a very dark place. The things that run through your mind are frightening, and what makes it worse is that nobody is there to bring you back to a healthy place mentally and spiritually. When you are in that place of isolation, you don't necessarily realize you are there because you begin to lose sight of what's around you. Isolation anesthetizes you from your current context, and you begin to normalize dysfunctional behavior.

Have you had moments in your life when you just didn't want to talk? You felt like coming home, turning off the lights, and pulling down the shades on the windows. Your belief was that you were shielding yourself from further pain and shielding others from seeing the pain that plagued you, but in reality you were providing the devil with a portal of access to torment you. Please be clear: there is nothing wrong with being alone. However, there is a vast difference between being alone and being in isolation. Oftentimes God will separate you and lead you in a time of aloneness to test you, but the devil will put you in isolation to torment you.

When Jesus was close to Calvary, He experienced one of the greatest tests of His life. Jesus went to Gethsemane to pray, and upon entering the place, He became sorrowful and heavy in heart, even to the point where His inner turmoil felt like death. His prayer to God was a plea to let the "cup" pass from Him. Jesus' drinking of the cup included fulfilling His earthly assignment to take on the sins of the world and die sacrificially so we could be reconciled to God. During this time of agony, Jesus questioned His location. Matthew 26:39 states, "And He went a little farther and fell on His face, and prayed, saying, O My Father, if it be possible, let this cup pass from Me: nevertheless, not as I will, but as You will."

Jesus endured a physical struggle with where He found Himself at that particular point in His life. When Jesus came to a place of surrender to the will of God, the Bible says that "an angel appeared to Him from heaven, strengthening Him. And being in agony, He prayed more earnestly. Then His sweat became like great drops of blood falling down to the ground" (Luke 22:43–44). Jesus was alone in that moment, and the agony was intense. But because He understood the necessity of His death, He did not forfeit the assignment. His surrender led to His being strengthened by the angel from heaven.

When you surrender to the will of God, you will be strengthened to endure the periods of aloneness, even when it feels like no one understands the totality of what you are going through. This is also important to note. Although the disciples were supposed to be partnered with Jesus, they fell asleep when they were supposed to be praying. Although they were physically with Jesus, they were not truly with Him in the sense that they were able to empathize with His internal struggle. The disconnection of the disciples was yet another reason Jesus could have given to make His case for feeling isolated. However, instead of complaining about the disciples' lack of commitment, He continued moving from this place of isolation so He could make it to Calvary, which was His final, and most important, earthly destination.

An important thing we must realize about Jesus' experience is that the alone time was designated for communing with God. It was not an attempt to shut God out. One way to determine whether your time of separation from people is part of a test from God or the devil's attempt to torment you is to understand how you got to that place of aloneness. Did the Spirit lead you there, or did the devil drive you there? If the Spirit of the Lord led you there, the period of aloneness is from God and will be temporary. When you are led into a state of aloneness, you are there only until you have completed the tests. Isolation, on the other hand, is designed to have long-term effects. The devil will drive you into a place of isolation in an effort to torment you forever. Isolation has no boundaries or limitations; the longer you stay, the deeper the darkness becomes.

In those early months after my wife's death I was invited out to various activities, and I kept declining because I had convinced myself that isolation was my safe place. Maybe you are going through a similar season where you have divested from certain people and places. I've been there. It's easy to convince yourself that you are fine being a committee of one. I didn't want to explain anything, nor was I interested in pretending I was OK when in actuality I wasn't. I would take long drives just to escape the demands of my schedule. I would purposely put my phone on Do Not Disturb. There were days when I didn't even check my mailbox, hoping people would assume I wasn't home. I just wanted to be left alone. This went on for nearly six months.

I later discovered that isolation was never a safe place for me but a satanic attack masked as safety. There were many times I was in settings with hundreds of people and still felt like I was alone because I was convinced nobody truly understood what I was dealing with. Many times, when you are hurting, you would rather hurt alone than hurt among those who have no idea of the depths of your pain. I didn't want to subject people to my unrealistic expectations, so I felt it was best to deal with my emotions alone.

What isolation produced in my mind were imaginations

and assumptions that I never should have allowed. I now understand Paul's instruction in 2 Corinthians 10:5: "…casting down imaginations, and every high thing that exalts against the knowledge of God, and bringing into captivity every thought to the obedience of Christ" (KJV). If these images running through your mind are not cast down, your isolation can thrust you into a false reality and a false sense of security where you become self-sufficient and suspicious of the intents of anyone who seeks to help you.

Maybe at times you conceptually knew you needed counseling but couldn't will yourself to go. Maybe you were in a bad relationship that pulled you into isolation. You knew the relationship was unhealthy, but you continued to justify your actions and tell yourself there was nothing wrong with the situation. People kept telling you how you seemed to have changed and that you were no longer associating with your friends, but you were so far gone, you didn't see a way to return to what used to be normalcy.

Isolation is so easy to fall into when you are under spiritual attack that you have to be aware of it, or you will fall prey to it. Isolation is given a license to control your life when places within you die. In discussing social isolation, one psychologist wrote that "humans are hardwired to interact with others, especially during times of stress. When we go through a trying ordeal alone, a lack of emotional support and friendship can increase our anxiety and hinder our coping ability."[1] The enemy seeks to convince us that we will be better working through our problems on our own, but we were not designed to work through traumatic experiences alone. We need help! Whether it is spiritual help, clinical help, or both, we need help coping with attacks that come upon us.

Failure to get help will leave you alone with only the devil speaking to you about your situation. This tormenting spirit does not want to see you healed. The devil wants to get you alone to speak to you so he can do damage beyond what you have already experienced. When the devil is the only being speaking to you, there is no one around you to let you know that what you are hearing, saying, or doing is not healthy behavior. Without people within your community around you, you lack a checks and balances system to help give you wise counsel regarding your thoughts, words, or actions. As Proverbs 11:14 says, "Where there is no counsel, the people fall; but in the multitude of counselors there is safety." You need people around you to ensure your thoughts are in line with the Word of God and the moral and ethical guidelines of society.

When you are in total isolation, you are the only one present to help you work through the ambiguous nature of what you are experiencing. Your hurt will not allow you to rationally think through the situation because your inward look will allow you to focus only on who hurt you, what hurt you, what happened, when it happened, and why it happened. It is difficult to find a solution to your situation when you have turned a deaf ear to any external assistance. If all you listen to is yourself and the voice of the enemy within, your state of mind will reflect only the hurt and pain you went through, therefore causing you more harm and quite possibly leading you to be hurtful to others. Hurt people hurt people, and if you are in a place without any consistent human interaction, when you do encounter others, your limited connections will reflect an interaction that is void of the typical care, courtesy, compassion, and control in human interaction. Like the man living in the tombs, your behavior will be uncontrollable because your isolation will prevent you from measuring your thoughts, words, and actions against healthy behavior.

Neuroscientist John T. Cacioppo, coauthor of *Loneliness: Human Nature and the Need for Social Connection*, reported that "lonely people tend to be more hostile. They tend to eat foods that have higher contents of sugar and fat. The lonely have greater resistance to blood flow in their veins, which can lead to high blood pressure. Saliva tests reveal that lonely people produce more cortisol, a stress hormone, over sustained periods."[2] He went on to say loneliness is "an aversive warning sign that's evolved to signal the need for change in order to restore something necessary for your genetic survival." It is a tool that "protects the individual from isolation."[3] You have been designed with a biological self-check system to help protect you from becoming isolated, but when the devil attacks you, the attacks are strategically created to bypass your genetic warning signs.

DON'T MAKE YOUR DWELLING AMONG THE DEAD

One thing that makes the narrative in Mark 5 so interesting is that the spirit in the man caused him to adapt to life in a cemetery. His dwelling was among the tombs. When we dwell among the dead, we become the personification of hopelessness and depression. We wander aimlessly throughout life without purpose. We exist but don't live the life God intended for us.

When you reside among the dead, there is no accountability because dead folk can't talk, hear, or see. Isolation pulls you away from the living and forces you into community with the dead. I've seen people under attack pulled into dead relationships that isolated them from the people who cared about them. If there are no voices of reason and revelation around you, your willingness to assimilate in graveyards intensifies. The tombs are memorials of what was. If you aren't careful, the enemy will have you so busy romancing seasons in your past that you are unable to embrace the future God has prepared. Nothing living hangs out with the dead. When the enemy attacks, he is determined to make you comfortable with dead jobs, dead relationships, dead finances, dead emotions, and a dead spiritual life.

When I was in isolation, everything around me was dead. My motivation, passion, and even purpose felt dead. Perhaps this is where you are. You are in isolation, and you are beginning to realize you are not there by accident. All your attempts to foster friendships have been frustrated by one excuse after the next. It can be very difficult when you realize Satan has targeted you in an attempt to rob you of God's best. It's not too late to come out of it. God wired us to be in community. From the beginning of time it has always been God's desire for us to be in community. Anything that seeks to pull us away from a healthy community is demonic. At the same time, communities that seek to keep away the people who need them most are also functioning in the interest of the enemy.

Many people reading about the man in Mark 5 overlook the fact that the community cast him away and sent him to live in the cemetery. The community's inability to deal with the man's spiritual issue caused him to be placed among those who were dead. Remember in chapter 1 I mentioned that people were often labeled based on their condition. He had become the man among the tombs. Once culture labels you, they then create an institutional reality consistent with the name they gave you. The cemetery was the structural symbol that reinforced the label the man had been given. It became a constant reminder that he was the dead one.

Nothing can be done for you, and as a consequence you have been placed among the dead. Every single day the cemetery reinforces the name culture gave you in an attempt to remind you that this is your reality and you are never coming out. This is why it is important that you are mindful of the environments you allow yourself to be placed in. Often the enemy will use those places to constantly reiterate the names culture has given you.

Sometimes people are living among the tombs but don't recognize their environment for what it is because it allows them to roam around. Unlike the man in the text, their restraints are not so visible as they are disclosed. These people have a hard time leaving their environment because they are convinced nothing is wrong with it. In either case, Jesus doesn't support life in the cemetery, which is why when He finds you in a state of cemetery living, He extends deliverance to you to ensure you can experience the life you were designed to live. Jesus wants to change your location and move you out of the dead place that Satan has trapped you in with his devices of torment.

When you are under spiritual attack, Satan is not just interested in your visiting the dead place. He desires that you take up residence. When you do this, you become like the man in Mark 5, and you make the tomb your place of dwelling. Once this happens, people begin to identify you with it. Tomb living becomes synonymous with your personhood. You will become known as the woman or man who lives in the tomb. But the label is counter to who God created you to be, and the dwelling place is counter to where God created you to dwell. You were never meant to live in a dead place.

In the Book of Genesis, God did two things when we were created: He breathed the breath of life into our beings so we could become living souls, and He placed us in a garden, a lively, growing, nourishing environment in which to dwell. God never intended for us to live on the earth in a dead state of being because the purpose for His breathing into us was to ensure we were constantly connected to His life-giving Spirit. When God gave all humanity dominion over the earth, He wanted to ensure that no physical space would serve as a place of captivity for the man and woman He created. However, the fall distorted the plan of God for humanity, and the world man and woman were given dominion over possessed the ability to hold us captive.

The good news is that on Calvary Jesus reversed the

curse and reset God's original plan, setting in motion the ability for me and you to no longer be subject to the bonds of Satan. Ephesians 4:8 declares, "Wherefore he saith, when he ascended up on high, he led captivity captive, and gave gifts unto men" (KJV). Captivity no longer has control over you, but you have to encounter the power of Jesus to discover this truth. Jesus has come to make you free, and according to John 8:36, "if the Son therefore shall make you free, ye shall be free indeed" (KJV).

It is only through the power of the Son of God, Jesus, that you will be made completely free of the bonds of Satan and oppressive forces. Your destiny on the earth never included an extended stay in bondage and isolation. You were not created to become comfortable at the cemetery. The only people who go for extended stays at the cemetery are the dead.

Living among the dead had significant implications in this Mark 5 man's life, and it has consequences for me and you. If you are reading this and wondering why you are attracting dead relationships in your life, it is probably a result of what many have concluded is your place of residence. When you dwell among the dead, you can get comfortable in a job that has no upward mobility. Dwelling among the tombs can cause you to fall into chronic complacency. It can cause you to justify dysfunctional relationships.

If you are comfortable around the dead, the assumption is that another dead thing won't bother you. The amazing thing about Jesus is that He's not in the business of accommodating or tolerating dead things. He declared in John 14:6, "I am the way, the truth, and the life." His encounter with the man in Mark 5 was not only to address the spiritual attack the man was experiencing but also to reconnect him to the living.

God's plan for your life includes your coming out of your place of isolation. For you to get out of that place, the Lord needs you to come out of the tombs and meet Him at the edge of your cemetery. It may be a far distance to get to Jesus, and it may take some work to get there, but once you begin making the first steps toward the Lord, you will be further away from tomb living and one step closer to your destination.

For too long your red dot on the map of your life has been dictated by the devil and his devices. Jesus wants to give you direction in your life. He wants to eliminate your wandering in circles. Jesus wants to redirect your location so you will end up in the place originally intended. One thing I learned about going to a specific store in the mall as opposed to going from store to store is that it matters what entrance you choose. Knowing which anchor store is closest to your desired location can get you to your desired location much faster. You don't have to go through life going in circles, aimlessly wandering in frustration as you attempt to get to your destination. Jesus is your anchor in life, and when you learn to enter your situation through Him, you will end up in the right location.

ROOT WORK

1. Do you feel like you are in the right location in life? If the answer is yes, where are you currently located on your spiritual journey? If the answer is no, what is causing you to be off course?

2. How do you combat frustrations associated with spiritual attacks that prevent you from being in your desired location? List at least three methods you use, or will use, to combat attacks against you.

3. Have you struggled with isolation? If the answer is yes, identify what caused you to be in that place.

4. Have people labeled you in a way that has caused you to disconnect? If so, list the labels that have been placed on you over the course of your life, and then beside each label write what God's Word says about you.

5. If you are in a dead place, what are three things you can do immediately that will move you to a place among the living?

CHAPTER 3

Interrogation:
The Enemy in Me

Now that we've discussed isolation, it is essential that we understand the next dimension of spiritual warfare. I call it interrogation. Isolation creates the perfect setting for interrogation. When Satan, in the form of a serpent, approached Eve in Genesis chapter 3, Adam was not around. With no one nearby, Satan had the opportunity to question the word God had given Adam, which ultimately led to Eve's failure to recognize God's authority over their lives.

The enemy is aware of the power of God's Word, which is why he will attempt to dilute the Word of God that has been sown in your life. If he succeeds, you will not have the faith to fight the attacks leveled against you. This is why you must not be discouraged by what you see. What you see can cause disillusionment. You have to shift from focusing on what you see to walking in what you know. David said in Psalm 119:11, "I have hidden your word in my heart that I might not sin against you" (NIV). The more Word you hold on to, the less power the enemy will have against you.

In Genesis 3:1 the serpent asked, "Has God indeed said,

'You shall not eat of every tree of the garden'?" In response the woman shared the directive God had given regarding what she and Adam were permitted to eat: "We may eat the fruit of the trees of the garden; but of the fruit of the tree which is in the midst of the garden, God has said, 'You shall not eat it, nor shall you touch it, lest you die'" (Gen. 3:2–3).

Satan then perverted the word of God, which gave Eve a different perspective on what would occur if she ate of the fruit. Satan gave her a half-truth. He told her, "Ye shall not surely die: for God doth know that in the day ye eat thereof, then your eyes shall be opened, and ye shall be as gods, knowing good and evil" (Gen. 3:4–5, KJV). This was a half-truth because Satan knew that if Eve and her husband, Adam, ate of the fruit, they would not die immediately, but they would no longer live forever. Death would be inevitable.

Satan's interrogation technique included tempting Eve with the possibility of being elevated, telling her that "ye shall be as gods." In his response to Eve, Satan also introduced her to three temptations we all must beware of: "the lust of the flesh, the lust of the eyes, and the pride of life—[which are] not of the Father but…of the world" (1 John 2:16). These temptations are of this world, not of God, and Satan introduced them to gain entry into the minds of God's people. Satan always will attempt to gain access to your body through your mind by getting you to succumb to one or all of the temptations of sin.

The Genesis 3 account goes on to tell us that when the woman saw that the prohibited tree was good for food (giving in to the lust of the eyes) and that it was a tree desirable to make one wise (giving in to the pride of life), her final step was to take the fruit and eat it (giving in to the lust of the flesh). Once this occurred, the temptation to sin, along with questioning God's word and authority, became a recurring way Satan would interrogate God's people in moments of isolation. His objective is to pull you further and further away from the truth.

We see this interrogation technique again when Satan tempted Jesus in Matthew 4:

> Then Jesus was led up by the Spirit into the wilderness to be tempted by the devil. And when He had fasted forty days and forty nights, afterward He was hungry. Now when the tempter came to Him, he said, "If You are the Son of God, command that these stones become bread."
>
> But He answered and said, "It is written, 'Man shall not live by bread alone, but by every word that proceeds from the mouth of God.'"
>
> Then the devil took Him up into the holy city, set Him on the pinnacle of the temple, and said to Him, "If You are the Son of God, throw Yourself down. For it is written: 'He shall give His angels charge over you,' and, 'In their hands they shall bear you up, lest you dash your foot against a stone.'"
>
> Jesus said to him, "It is written again, 'You shall not tempt the Lord your God.'"
>
> Again, the devil took Him up on an exceedingly high mountain, and showed Him all the kingdoms of the world and their glory. And he said to Him, "All these things I will give You if You will fall down and worship me."

> Then Jesus said to him, "Away with you, Satan!
> For it is written, 'You shall worship the Lord your
> God, and Him only you shall serve.'" Then the devil
> left Him, and behold, angels came and ministered
> to Him.
>
> —MATTHEW 4:1–11

Jesus had been fasting and was presumably physically weak, and that's when the enemy interrogated Him concerning the Word. Jesus' counter to the interrogation was to declare, "It is written." By overcoming the temptations of sin Satan presented, Jesus reset humanity's response to satanic interrogation techniques, exposing them for what they truly are. Jesus was able to identify Satan for who he was. When you cannot identify the devil, you stand the chance of being charmed by someone or something that is actually Satan in disguise. Eve did not recognize the serpent as the devil. Because of this she allowed sin to enter her mind, and subsequently Satan gained access to her home and the world in which she lived. During His confrontation with the devil in Matthew 4, Jesus took the cover off Satan's tactics and schemes and revealed the true nature of temptation. He reestablished the course of destiny for believers by demonstrating how to overcome Satan's devices. If you are going to overcome the interrogation of Satan, you must declare God's Word over your life.

Respond to Satan's lies with what God has spoken. And when you declare the Word, decree that it is established. You cannot be timid when speaking God's Word over your situation. You must do so with authority, knowing the words you speak are the promises of God. Proverbs 18:21 reminds us, "The tongue has the power of life and death, and those who love it will eat its fruit" (NIV). Too many people speak death over their lives rather than declaring the living Word. When I was a child, my parents gave me a toy called a See 'n Say. This toy taught me various sounds from the animal kingdom. It had an arrow that could be turned to point to different animals, and there was a string attached to the toy. When the string was pulled, the toy would play the sound of the animal to which the arrow was pointing.

The makers of the toy programmed words into it, and the only way to get the words out was to pull the string. God has allowed you and me to be full of His Word, and often it's when Satan pulls our strings that the Word emerges with power. Perhaps Satan has pulled your string by attacking your health. You must declare that by Jesus' stripes you are healed (1 Pet. 2:21–25). Maybe he has pulled your string regarding your finances. Declare and decree that your God will supply every one of your needs according to His riches in heaven (Phil. 4:19). Don't sit back and succumb to the attacks upon your life. Open your mouth and declare God's Word.

On a personal note, when I lost my first wife, the enemy taunted me in isolation. There were moments I would question my anointing. Satan said to me, "You've prayed over others and they recovered. Why didn't it work with your wife?" On the day she passed, Satan questioned me concerning the legitimacy of God's Word. I remembered the words of Job when he was experiencing his personal ordeal, and I found the strength to declare as he did, "Though he slay me, yet will I trust in him: but I will maintain mine own ways before him" (Job 13:15, KJV). But the interrogation occurred daily with the sole purpose of causing me to lose focus and flirt with depression.

Perhaps you are going through interrogation right now. The demons are telling you it's your fault or you should have done more. The enemy may be telling you that you were too friendly or too trusting. Maybe the enemy is telling you that you were too weak and that your relationship with God is only a facade. You are rehearsing what happened over and over in your mind, trying to figure out what went wrong. You can't beat yourself up and allow Satan to cause you to live in a constant state of blame and shame. You have to remember what God's Word has promised you regardless of what the demons attempt to say to you. Remember to talk back to the enemy, knowing that God's Word is more trustworthy than any words the enemy is speaking to you during warfare.

Interrogation is designed to make you feel inadequate and convince you that you failed. I had moments when I questioned my call and the anointing upon my life. Can you imagine preaching for years and telling people God can heal, only to have your own wife die of sickness? Satan wanted me to believe my prayers weren't enough to prevent the death of my wife, and there were Sundays when I didn't want to go to the pulpit because I lived in shame. I felt people doubted the authenticity of what I preached and believed. This is how interrogation works.

It seeks to weaken your witness and cause you to second-guess your faith.

SATAN ATTACKS FROM THE INSIDE OUT

When you are experiencing this level of attack, you have to understand that the enemy wants to control your mind, body, and spirit. For the man in the tombs, at some point in his life something went awry on the inside. After the unclean spirit took up residence inside him, he no longer had control over the workings of his mind or the actions of his body, and his spirit became governed by demons, which means he was disconnected from God's Spirit.

Spiritual warfare is an attack from the inside out. If you don't understand that, you will attempt to fight it from the outside in. Demons have always sought a vessel to invade. Satan entered a snake in Genesis and continues to seek refuge in us. This is why you have to be careful of the portals you keep open in your life. These portals allow demonic access and encroachment. It is very important that you understand that Christians cannot be possessed by demons. A demon cannot invade where the Holy Spirit resides. Only in unbelievers is this possible. Yet as believers we have to be aware that the enemy can suppress us. The enemy can use warfare to frustrate the plans of God for our lives. In both instances the enemy seeks access.

One tool the enemy loves to use to create openings in our spirits to gain access to our lives is offense. The devil is looking for somebody hurt enough, mad enough, bitter enough, desperate enough, or tired enough. I've heard it said that we should be careful and pay close attention to the acronym HALT because whenever we are hungry, angry, lonely, or tired, the enemy looks for opportunities to attack us. The enemy wants to exploit us in our weakest moments. The enemy attacked Jesus after He had fasted and was hungry. I've experienced my greatest attacks when I was exhausted from a day of multiple obligations. When you've poured out, it's critical that you take the time to allow the Lord to pour back into you so you are not left exposed to the plots and schemes of the enemy.

When we are on empty, we are more susceptible to satanic exploitation. We often react rather than take our time and respond. The reality is that our reactions often have long-term, negative consequences in the lives of those who encounter us. When you reflect on your life, I'm sure you can remember times when you gave the enemy access because you were not guarding your emotions. It happens to the best of us. Everybody has had experiences when we cracked the door to the devil and in some instances left the door wide open. Maybe there were times when you worked to the point of exhaustion or times you were betrayed by a confidant. These moments are not to be taken lightly because the enemy will seize them to wage a spiritual attack on your life.

The demonic spirits that have you in a state of inter-rogation may come in different forms. You may not be living on the outskirts of the city or placed in physical restraints like the man in Mark 5, but the internal conflict resulting from your engagement with the devil will leave you ostracized to some degree. This may mean you are excluded from social activities and people distance themselves from you in social settings. It may also be evident in the way your friends, family, and coworkers communicate with you, especially if the interrogation has caused you to become defensive and think every encounter you have with others is an interrogation as well.

If every time someone asks, "How are you doing?" you respond with suspicion or combative questions, you will be placed on the outskirts of your social sphere, which will bring further emotional damage. This distancing from others will also cause spiritual harm because believers are strengthened by being in community with others. To those who are in the midst of interrogation, please know that everyone is not out to get you. If you are in a space of constant fear, frustration, doubt, and disillusionment, you may need to be freed from the clutches of the enemy, who is conducting an illegal interrogation process on you.

Legal experts have told me of interrogation techniques that cause suspects in cases to confess to things of which they may not be guilty. These techniques include accusing, yelling, invading the individuals' space, and lying about evidence against them.[1] Satan uses bullying and deceptive tactics too. He will attempt to push you into a place where you feel so threatened by the forces coming against you that you accept a life sentence of torment you were never meant to serve. But if you are in a state of interrogation, there is hope. You can be freed from being perpetually accused and badgered for mistakes that have already been forgiven. The key to deliverance is to demonstrate authority when it comes to encountering the unclean spirits. If you have accepted

Christ as your Savior, every spirit that is not the Spirit of God must leave you. The enemy cannot abide where the power of God resides.

If, however, you don't know the authority you have been given, the enemy can gain a foothold in your life. And once the enemy gains access, the interrogation will escalate. The unclean spirit will attempt to control how you process the Word in your life. If the enemy is successful in doing this, he can create a narrative that makes you think the consequences of sin and dysfunction are not so bad. Satan does this because he wants to reconstruct your reality. If he can keep you from living in the truth of the Word, he can keep you from the freedom you were meant to have.

This reminds me of a humorous story I once heard about the duck church. One Sunday the duck pastor stood before his congregation to preach and announced the title of his sermon: "Why Walk When You Can Fly?" The duck pastor preached passionately and with much conviction, impressing upon the duck congregation the possibilities that were before them. The sermon was received with rousing duck applause, and after the service all the ducks got up and walked home.

The moral of this story is that you can have all the Word and faith in the world, but if they don't manifest in your works, they are dead. I've seen people attend church faithfully, hear the Word, and take lots of notes, yet they were unable to handle the demons that had attacked their lives. There are people who work in ministry and do amazing things for the kingdom yet have difficulty overcoming the inward attacks of the enemy. This frequently occurs because people can come to church week after week yet be what I refer to as "functional Christians."

Functional or high-functioning Christians are those who are accustomed to doing church work and are learned in the Word of God and the works of the Lord; however, they have difficulty applying what they learn because of the attachments of the unclean spirits affecting their lives. The unclean spirits seek to occupy and suppress so much space that there is no room for the life-changing Word to come in and do something new. Denial that they have any issues also keeps these believers from receiving new revelation for their lives, and consequently they do not apply the Word they hear on Sunday or Wednesday. The inability to apply the Word of God correlates with their inability to admit they are experiencing demonic interrogation. What we see occurring in high-functioning Christians is similar to a functional or high-functioning alcoholic. Functional alcoholics suffer from alcohol use disorder. Externally they seem to have everything together, but internally they are battling to even admit they have a problem that needs to be addressed.

According to medical research, "functional alcoholics may seem to be in control...but they may put themselves or others in danger by drinking and driving, having risky sexual encounters, or blacking out."[2] Like those trying to function while in the grips of addiction, people driven to maintain a certain external facade while experiencing an internal struggle end up going deeper into their own world of hurt and pain and further away from people who could help lead them to the source of their healing.

THE ENEMY WITHIN

The enemy is truly in me. It's difficult to deal with an internal struggle because what most people see is the external manifestation. They see the anger, bitterness, low self-esteem, or the emotional instability. It's easy to make judgment calls when you see a particular action. But the real enemy is within. I remember my father telling me to sweep down the spiderwebs on the side of our home when I was a kid. I swept every wall, gate, and object that was in sight. After I cleared all the spiderwebs, something interesting occurred. They were back the next day. My dad told me that sweeping spiderwebs is a futile exercise. It doesn't matter how careful you are while sweeping—if you don't kill the spiders, you will constantly deal with their webs. We live in a world that is consumed with treating symptoms while neglecting to address the source. We can suppress a symptom, but that does nothing to eradicate the cause.

The interrogation that occurs within us is a result of the spirit that has taken up residence and is able to hide, sometimes for years, without being noticed. We aren't sure how long the man in Mark 5 had been in the tomb, but we can assume it had been some time considering the numerous attempts that had been made to tie him up or tame him. The community had exerted much energy dealing with the outward manifestations he presented. What this suggests is that the spirit within the man was able to go unaddressed for years. Though the community knew the man had an unclean spirit, their approach was to remedy his actions rather than deal with what caused them. Within us all there are things that have gone unaddressed. You can know they are there but not know how to address them. This is how the enemy interrogates you. You can function at high levels and create an image while internally struggling with a spirit that constantly torments you.

These enemies within could be pornography, substance abuse, or other addictive or ungodly behaviors that threaten your destiny. When these enemies are active in your life, Satan, who is the enemy of all believers, uses your entertainment of the enemies within you to bring accusations against you. Revelation 12:10 tells us that at the end there will be "a loud voice saying in heaven, Now is come salvation, and strength, and the kingdom of our God, and the power of his Christ: for the accuser of our brethren is cast down, which accused them before our God day and night" (KJV). Satan sends the enemies and designs the struggles that come against you, and his agenda includes accusing you day and night.

The apostle Paul shed light on this internal interrogation and struggle:

> For we know that the law is spiritual, but I am carnal, sold under sin. For what I am doing, I do not understand. For what I will to do, that I do not practice; but what I hate, that I do. If, then, I do what I will not to do, I agree with the law that it is good. But now, it is no longer I who do it, but sin that dwells in me. For I know that in me (that is, in my flesh) nothing good dwells; for to will is present with me,

but how to perform what is good I do not find. For the good that I will to do, I do not do; but the evil I will not to do, that I practice. Now if I do what I will not to do, it is no longer I who do it, but sin that dwells in me. I find then a law, that evil is present with me, the one who wills to do good. For I delight in the law of God according to the inward man. But I see another law in my members, warring against the law of my mind, and bringing me into captivity to the law of sin which is in my members. O wretched man that I am! Who will deliver me from this body of death? I thank God—through Jesus Christ our Lord! So then, with the mind I myself serve the law of God, but with the flesh the law of sin.

—ROMANS 7:14–25

This internal civil war that Paul described is not unfamiliar to any of us. It's easy to point to an enemy on the outside, but the enemy is really within. This spirit attaches itself to carnality, where it is more comfortable manifesting. It dwells in your carnality to weigh down your spiritual life and hides within you in an attempt to avoid accountability. By dwelling in your carnality, this spirit is aware that you will not have strength to fight off other spirits because it will cause your carnal nature to overpower your spirit. I am convinced that carnality works from the inside out. It starts in the mind and manifests in our members. In Galatians 5:17 Paul helps to shed light on this internal battle, stating, "For the flesh lusteth against the Spirit, and the Spirit against the flesh: and these are contrary the one to the other: so that ye cannot do the things that ye would" (KJV).

The internal struggles and interrogations we experience are quite common among believers. The assumption is often that Christians don't have these struggles. Many people go through life pretending they don't exist. As I shared earlier in this book, it's easy to present a perception about yourself and an image to feed it. Many of the moral casualties we have experienced in the kingdom could have been prevented had people felt comfortable dealing with the enemy within them.

Because the church has a tendency to make some sins seem worse than others, people often are not inclined to address their internal demons until it's too late. The moral hierarchism tragically at work in the church allows people to condemn others while seeking grace for their own sin. Paul courageously shared his experience in Romans 7 so all of us could find a point of identification. Paul demonstrated that, as the young people say, "The struggle is real." If we continue to allow this unclean spirit to torment and interrogate us, we will never experience the freedom Jesus has come to bring.

Maybe you are experiencing the spiritual warfare of interrogation right now. The unclean spirit is telling you, "You will never be free," or, "Accept this as your new normal." You have to believe the report of the Lord concerning your life. When spirits have invaded your life, true deliverance can never occur unless you allow God's Holy Spirit to fill you completely, making no room for the enemy.

When I was young, I learned a powerful lesson from a simple life experience. There were specks of debris in my glass of water. I was attempting to get them out with my hand, but I was painfully unsuccessful. When my father saw my frustration, he helped me remove the debris. He put the glass under the faucet and let the water run into the glass until it overflowed. As the water continued to run into the glass, the debris rose to the top and came out.

The only way the spirits within us will be exposed and brought out is if we allow the Holy Spirit to fill us completely, until we overflow with presence and power and there is no room for anything unlike Him to take up residence in our lives. No matter what you have been facing and no matter what the enemy has told you during his interrogation, you can be victorious because the Scripture says, "Greater is he that is in you, than he that is in the world" (1 John 4:4, KJV).

ROOT WORK

1. Have you ever experienced demonic interrogation?

2. Whenever you have been under spiritual attack, what areas of your life were targeted?

3. What measures do you have in place that will prevent you from experiencing further loss in your life as a result of spiritual attacks?

4. Has the fear of being judged prevented you from revealing what you are going through? If yes, how can you overcome this fear to begin the process of living in truth?

5. How do you plan to block Satan's access to your life going forward?

CHAPTER 4

Situation:
I Tried It and It Didn't Work

ONE OF THE most intriguing things about the story in Mark 5 is that those in the community who sought to tie the man with chains and tame the spirit were unsuccessful. Mark 5:3–4 says, "And no one could bind him, not even with chains, because he had often been bound with shackles and chains. And the chains had been pulled apart by him, and the shackles broken in pieces; neither could anyone tame him." This gives us insight into the man's situation, which was not so different from yours and mine. The demons we are dealing with have created a great deal of frustration for us and those who have sought to assist us, because unclean spirits are not compliant. Demons are rebellious and committed to completing their evil intent in your life, and they will resist efforts to stop them.

I remember ministering to a mother who was at her wits' end with her son. He had become rebellious and refused to do what she asked. He was hanging out with the wrong crowd and engaging in behavior that often put his life in jeopardy. His teachers didn't know what to do. Various counselors had recommended things for this mother to do, but nothing worked. When she came to see me, she was beyond frustrated. It was clear we were dealing with a spirit in her son that was determined to be disruptive and disobedient.

My heart went out to this mother because I could see the beginning of what a broken heart looks like. When we are being victimized by demons, we often are oblivious to the collateral damage we are causing along the way. This mother wanted a solution to this problem and had come to me in a last-ditch effort. What I shared with her is what I will share with you. Your faith must transcend your frustration. I know it may be a difficult time for you. I know you keep hitting a brick wall. I know you have exhausted time and resources, but you cannot lose hope based on what has gone wrong in the past. Too much is at stake for you to resign yourself to think this is the way it will always be. You have an amazing future, and it's worth fighting for. Don't let the fear of failure cause you to forfeit your deliverance.

You have the power to overcome any attacks that come against your life, whether the attacks are direct or indirect. The indirect attacks often come through family members or close friends who are being manipulated by demonic spirits. That situation can make you feel hopeless because you may feel that your hands are tied in the situation if the person does not desire to be delivered. But you must remember there is nothing too hard for God. Deliverance in some situations requires a stronger strategy.

In Mark 9 we witness the deliverance of a young man

who had been under demonic attack since he was a young child. His father brought him to Jesus after others had failed to expel the demon, including Jesus' disciples. The Scriptures state:

> Then one of the crowd answered and said, "Teacher, I brought You my son, who has a mute spirit. And wherever it seizes him, it throws him down; he foams at the mouth, gnashes his teeth, and becomes rigid. So I spoke to Your disciples, that they should cast it out, but they could not."
>
> He answered him and said, "O faithless generation, how long shall I be with you? How long shall I bear with you? Bring him to Me." Then they brought him to Him. And when he saw Him, immediately the spirit convulsed him, and he fell on the ground and wallowed, foaming at the mouth.
>
> So He asked his father, "How long has this been happening to him?"
>
> And he said, "From childhood. And often he has thrown him both into the fire and into the water to destroy him. But if You can do anything, have compassion on us and help us."
>
> Jesus said to him, "If you can believe, all things are possible to him who believes."
>
> Immediately the father of the child cried out and said with tears, "Lord, I believe; help my unbelief!"
>
> When Jesus saw that the people came running together, He rebuked the unclean spirit, saying to it, "Deaf and dumb spirit, I command you, come out of him and enter him no more!" Then the spirit cried

out, convulsed him greatly, and came out of him. And he became as one dead, so that many said, "He is dead." But Jesus took him by the hand and lifted him up, and he arose.

And when He had come into the house, His disciples asked Him privately, "Why could we not cast it out?"

So He said to them, "This kind can come out by nothing but prayer and fasting."

—MARK 9:17–29

Deliverance is available to you and those connected to you. But conquering the crisis in your life may call for a shift in your strategy. You cannot expect others to do for you what God has empowered you to do for yourself. Too many believers adopt a strategy of codependence. Our relationship with Christ should shift us to walk in the reality of what He declared in John 14:12: "The works that I do he will do also; and greater works than these he will do, because I go to my Father." You've been given authority, so you must walk in it with confidence and declare God's Word over your situation. Commit more time to fasting and prayer, and you will experience the results you desire.

Whatever you are facing, you have to remember to remain full of faith and not lose hope. Jesus provided these words of hope in John 16:33: "These things I have spoken to you, that in Me you may have peace. In the world you will have tribulation; but be of good cheer, I have overcome the world." Jesus has already overcome everything you could possibly experience in the world; therefore, you do not have to remain as one who is without help. Instead, do as the Bible instructs in Hebrews 4:16 and "come boldly to the throne of grace, that [you] may obtain mercy and find grace to help in time of need." You no longer have to be a victim of your circumstances, but you can be a victor through Christ.

AVOIDING SETBACKS

If you've ever dealt with someone who was under demonic attack, you should know firsthand the challenges that come with trying to get the person to a healthy place. If you have personally been under attack and had numerous failed attempts at deliverance, you also understand the frustration associated with it. One thing we must acknowledge about the unclean spirit in the man in the tombs is that it was a resistant spirit. It was a rebellious spirit. It was a spirit intent on normalizing the dysfunctional environment it had created for itself.

When you are dealing with spiritual warfare similar to what we see in this man among the tombs, you have to prepare yourself for setbacks on the way to success. It is important to understand something about demons in general and the setbacks they cause. Setbacks often arise because the rebellious spirit seeks to return to the place where it had taken up residence. We will discover later in the book how the demon in the man among the tombs attempted to negotiate remaining in the region after being cast out. For now I want you to realize that unless something is filling the space the demon previously occupied, the unclean spirit will take up residence once again and will strive to bring other spirits along with it. This is just the nature of demons. Jesus provided a depiction of how this setback can occur:

> When an unclean spirit goes out of a man, he goes through dry places, seeking rest, and finds none. Then he says, "I will return to my house from which I came." And when he comes, he finds it empty, swept, and put in order. Then he goes and takes with him seven other spirits more wicked than himself, and they enter and dwell there; and the last state of that man is worse than the first. So shall it also be with this wicked generation.
>
> —Matthew 12:43–45

When you are engaged in spiritual warfare, not only must you command the unclean spirit to leave, but you must also prevent its reentry by knowing how and with what things to fill your spiritual house. (I will speak more about this in chapter 7.) According to 1 Corinthians 6:19, our bodies are the temple of the Holy Spirit. The temple of the Holy Spirit should be filled only with God's Spirit and the fruit of His Spirit. In their book *Pigs in the Parlor: The Practical Guide to Deliverance* Frank and Ida Hammond stated that "for each demon that is cast out, the gifts and fruits of the Holy Spirit must replace it. This is the express responsibility of the delivered person."[1] The fruit of the Spirit according to Galatians 5:22–23 "is love, joy, peace, longsuffering, gentleness, goodness, faith, meekness, temperance" (KJV).

I remember having an oil leak in my car that I

procrastinated getting fixed. It would leave the nastiest oil spots in my garage. I would find myself spending hours trying to remove the oil stains from my garage floor. This was a fruitless exercise because as long as I was avoiding the real problem, I would always have an oil stain on my garage floor. When I decided to deal with the problem and get the leak fixed, I was able to see a change.

We often address the cosmetic realities of our lives in an attempt to appear clean when in fact we have spiritual leaks that allow unclean spirits to stain us. In her book *Clean House—Strong House* Pastor Kimberly Daniels compared the removal of the unclean spirits to the "after-birth" that is delivered after a woman gives birth to a child. She stated, "Anything from your past to which you return as a source is a type of *spiritual afterbirth*. It is poisonous and contaminated!"[2]

When you examine the community's attempt to tie the man up, what becomes apparent is that numerous people attempted to bind him with no success. When one effort failed, another was applied. This reveals two things about spiritual warfare. The first is that the spirits adapted to whatever expertise was brought to the situation and were able to outwit it. It is probable that the community sent in experts who specialized in binding people in chains, but the demons learned to adapt. It's similar to predators in the wild who have adapted to the venom of their prey. Over time they develop immunity to it. In each attempt to tie him up, the man kept breaking the chains. The second thing this reveals to us is that the demons not only broke the chains but also destroyed them to discourage any future attempts. It appears in the text that in time the people gave up trying to tie the man up.

This is the ultimate aim of the spirit you are dealing with. The spirit wants to roam unhindered by anything or anyone. It wants to bring you to a point of resignation so you will no longer seek to overcome it. This spirit can invade your marriage and frustrate all your attempts to make it work and conform to the image of Christ. You go to counseling and see no change. You attend marriage conferences, and the problems remain. You've tried one thing after the next, and nothing seems to work. This is not the time to throw in the towel; this is the time to recognize your warfare for what it is. The enemy isn't playing around with you, and you can't be passive when dealing with a demon. Your faith has to be as stubborn as the spirit you are dealing with. So many people have just given up all hope that things will change because of the numerous attempts that didn't work. They are living in misery and madness because, after trying one thing after another, they allowed the demonic spirit to prevail over them.

Have you considered another approach? Those in the community continued to use chains or fetters. If you continue doing the same thing over and over, you will get the same results. I've seen many people institute programs in their churches in an attempt to address the difficult situations in which people find themselves. I've also witnessed how stubborn people can be when things don't work. Rather than attempt something new, they bring another "chain" to the situation. Instead of seeking to understand the individuals and the issues at the root, they attempt to control them. What Jesus' presence represented was a new approach to an old problem. Perhaps God is asking us to revisit our approaches and find others who are being successful and connect with them. When we research best practices, we are able to gain victories much more easily than when we do things by ourselves.

Sometimes you have to leave the land of the Gadarenes to see how other people are dealing with their demons. If our methodologies are the result of limited exposure, we don't do ourselves justice. Talk to other people who have had similar challenges. Seek out what has helped others move closer to healing. Their path may not be identical to yours, but there is much we can learn from one another. We often get comfortable in our context, using systems that don't work, and fail to explore other options. When I was a child, I had a wonderful toy called an Etch A Sketch. It had two knobs at the bottom that when turned would draw lines to create the images you desired. I enjoyed drawing homes. One day I messed up, and my lines went too far in one direction. My natural proclivity was to turn the knobs in the opposite direction. Upon doing so, I quickly realized that was not the solution. The lines reversed and retraced the previous line that was made in error. My father took the toy from me and shook it, and when he did so, the screen became clear again. I was able to start over.

Maybe that's a lesson for you today. Rather than go back and repeat crooked lines or ineffective methods, allow God to shake things up and give you a fresh approach. Whenever I need to find a fresh approach, I remind myself of God's words through the prophet Isaiah: "Do not remember the former things, nor consider the things of old. Behold, I will do a new thing, now it shall spring forth; shall you not know it? I will even make a road in the wilderness and rivers in the desert" (43:18–19).

Behold, God will do a new thing—and He will show you a new strategy for defeating the enemy that is attacking you. But you must keep in mind that deliverance is not a sprint; it's a marathon. There will be good days and bad. There will be successes and failures. Just because you tried one of the strategies in this book and did not see results does not mean it will never bear fruit. What I share in this book are some proven strategies that work, but deliverance can take time. Many people are looking for a quick remedy when in fact we must be willing to go through the sometimes arduous process that leads to deliverance. A quick-fix approach absolves us of any responsibility. Some people just want deliverance to happen without putting in any effort. What you are dealing with didn't come quickly. It came in your life over time. This is not a new demon; it's been around a while. Solomon told us in Ecclesiastes 1:9, "That which has been is what will be, that which is done is what will be done, and there is nothing new under the sun." You are not the first person to be attacked by an unclean spirit, and this demon is not new to attacking people. In many cases the demons have been around for generations. The demons you are facing now are some of the same demons that tormented your parents and grandparents. In some cases the demon may have been affecting your family for several generations.

Don't beat yourself up if you tried to abandon certain practices and fell back into former patterns. Don't give up if you put your best foot forward and found yourself regressing into old ways. When the children of Israel experienced deliverance, it was after Moses made several visits to the Pharaoh's palace to petition him for their release. Deliverance requires work, but when we are persistent, it will come. I've said on numerous occasions that success does not come by the elevator; it comes by the stairs. You have to take one step at a time.

When thinking about deliverance as a process, not an event, consider the following analogy. Imagine eating vanilla ice cream all your life. Then when you become an adult, you are told that instead of eating vanilla ice cream you should eat chocolate. You put down vanilla and pick up chocolate. You develop a taste for chocolate and tell all your friends that you are done with vanilla. This goes on for a few weeks, but one night something interesting happens. You start craving vanilla.

You know you shouldn't eat it, but you can't shake the desire. You try to tame your appetite, but it continues to grow. To remedy your craving, you eat swirl. You now have mixed some vanilla with your chocolate. This is what most Christians experience along the process of deliverance. I call it the swirl stage. That's when your failures are blending with your successes. Though this story may be somewhat humorous, the point of it is this: as you mature in the process, there should be less and less vanilla in your chocolate.

Maybe you are reading this and you've been down on yourself because you continue to experience failures in your attempt to be free of your inner struggles. Perhaps shame has set in and you don't feel worthy of even going to church, so you've chosen to just stay home. Remember, this is the plot of the enemy to keep you in isolation. Let me be the first to tell you that you are not in this by yourself. We've all tried and come up short. You don't have to live in condemnation. Romans 8:1 says, "There is therefore now no condemnation to them which are in Christ Jesus, who walk not after the flesh, but after the Spirit" (KJV). The blessing is that we live another day to try again.

A CHAIN MINDSET

Let's take a moment to revisit the chains the people in the community used to address the spirit plaguing the man. I am convinced there was a certain mentality among those in the Gadarenes that exists among many today. It's a chain mentality. What causes people to choose an oppressive mechanism as a remedy? Too many use a nonredemptive approach to deliverance that is in conflict with the teaching of Jesus. Rather than use a model that liberates the man, they seek to tie him up further. As I mentioned earlier, the man was already tied up internally by a demon. Now he was tied up externally by those in his community. This approach did not work then, and it won't work now. I pray this revelation leads us to practice restoring and not restraining.

Our justice system is an example of how we as a society have practiced putting chains on people and isolating them in places such as jails and prisons. We have created social systems designed to bind people instead of seeking methods to restore those who are engaged in behavior that often leads to criminal acts, especially when the behavior begins when they are teenagers or young adults. Although many situations merit harsh consequences with regard to criminal activity, there are countless cases where a different approach would bring about a more restorative result.

People who are plagued by systematic oppression caused by social inequities such as unequal education and impoverished neighborhoods that are riddled with crime, drugs, and sex trafficking more frequently find themselves in the criminal justice system. Over the years as a pastor I have sat in courtrooms and visited jails and prisons to support my church members or the relatives of members when they found themselves face to face with the legal system. One of the most critical cases I have been intimately involved in is that of Cyntoia Brown, whose case has received national attention over the past few years.

Her story was both tragic and complicated. A victim of sex trafficking, prostitution, and abuse, Cyntoia Brown was found guilty of murder and sentenced to life in prison, having been tried as an adult for a crime she committed in 2004 at the age of sixteen. In December 2018 her case was appealed to the Tennessee Supreme Court, which ruled that she would be eligible for release after she serves fifty-one years in prison. I met the governor shortly after he took office, and I had worked on a few of his initiatives that were important to us both. We had been friends for seven years and had a mutual respect. I felt I was in a pivotal position to speak to him concerning this case. I requested a phone call with him in the eleventh hour of his tenure as governor. So many people had petitioned for Cyntoia's release, and her amazing legal team had worked tirelessly on her appeals and were in constant contact with the governor. I chose to add my voice to a chorus of others advocating for her future.

On January 7, 2019, the governor decided to grant her clemency. I was honored to play a small role alongside so many others in advocating for this. I share this to provide a further understanding of my desire to see people like Cyntoia given a second chance at life. She was a teenager who had experienced much abuse in her life, and as a result she became caught up in a situation that led to her committing a criminal act through which a life was lost and she was imprisoned. Her conviction, like countless others', is part of a larger systemic problem with incarcerating people who are often defenseless against the social ills of their community and end up engaging in criminal activity because they see no other options. According to Michelle Alexander, author of *The New Jim Crow*, "Mass incarceration is designed to warehouse a population deemed disposable—unnecessary to the functioning of the new global economy."[3] People who are deemed disposable, like the man in the tombs, are placed on the margins, put in chains or handcuffs, and made to live in the dead places of our prison systems.

There is a need for social reform to take place, more specifically in systems that seek to chain and contain instead of helping to restore those who have endured broken situations that have led to a life in bonds. Restorative justice practices that enable people to reenter society and become productive citizens must be considered. Restorative justice practices would be a sign of hope to people that they can move toward a better future, unlike traditional justice practices that view those who violate the law or moral codes of society as a hindrance to the community's progress.

My belief in the power of restoration over simple restraint led me to be an advocate for Cyntoia Brown's clemency. As we look forward to her release in August 2019, my church and I plan to give her our full support as she enters the next phase of her life. We will walk with her through her years of probation, help her with job placement, and assist her in her efforts to be a voice for others who endured some of the same hardships.

Cyntoia's case is just one example of how the current systems in place allowed for only one way of handling a person deemed disposable—to put them in bondage and lock them up. Yet the question must be asked, If that method is successful, why do our prisons continue to expand? If we truly desire to restore order to our communities, cities, states, nation, and world, we must be intentional about our efforts to combat the forces of darkness that come against the world in which we live.

Dealing with spiritual warfare is the responsibility of not just the individual but also the community at large. The church must be careful not to replicate the model of the Gadarenes. When we tie people up, it is an attempt to control. Remember, this is the community that put the man in the tombs. He was tied up and placed out of sight. They knew he was out there, but to maintain normalcy in their community, the people felt he needed to be in a contained environment. The church is guilty of this as well. We push things away or sweep them under the rug in an attempt to maintain what we hold sacred. Yet we run the risk of sacrificing the deliverance of our brothers and sisters to keep from disrupting our "sacred" systems. We have no idea how many people are hurting privately among us but are being pushed away because we don't like their issues. We are attempting to tie them down so they won't interrupt our way of existing. It should be apparent by now that when dealing with spiritual warfare, chains don't work.

If this man's situation does anything, it should cause us to reevaluate our approaches in dealing with those who are under spiritual attack. Like the mother I mentioned at the beginning of this chapter who was frustrated with her son's rebellion, we must be willing to persevere through the process while seeking new approaches. Never lose hope.

And rather than tying people up and pushing them away, perhaps we should consider welcoming them into the community and working together toward bringing them to a place of healing and wholeness. Too many good people are suffering in silence because we have adopted the approach of the people of the Gadarenes. The things we've tried for years haven't worked. Perhaps God is using this moment to awaken a fresh vision in your church or ministry to reach those who are hurting and bound. They are not disposable to God; they are dearly loved.

ROOT WORK

1. Have you ever dealt with someone who was under demonic attack? What was the most frustrating part of your encounters with the person?

2. Are you personally under demonic attack? If so, what are the most challenging aspects of the attack?

3. What approaches have you tried to rid yourself or a person close to you of demonic suppression?

4. If you have ever experienced setbacks in deliverance, what steps did you take to get back on track?

5. How does your faith community deal with spiritual warfare? List some ways it can improve, if you see any.

CHAPTER 5

Manifestation:
I'm Doing This to Myself

A S WE CONTINUE to learn lessons from the man living among the tombs, understanding how spirits manifest is one of the most important. It is a fact that whatever is in us will eventually come out of us. The unclean spirit that invaded this man's life manifested in some unusual ways. Mark 5:5 says, "And always, night and day, he was in the mountains and in the tombs, crying out and cutting himself with stones." One of the tactics of Satan is to get you to do things he is too cowardly or powerless to do. Self-destructive behavior presents itself when we participate in things that destroy our destiny or threaten our lives.

We are often made to believe certain behavior will lessen the reality or intensity of our struggle. I've seen people drink themselves into a frenzy in an attempt to drown their problems. They soon discovered that their problems knew how to swim. Others have used drugs or narcotics in an attempt to get high enough to leave their problems behind, but they soon discovered that their problems knew how to fly as well. Whether it is dysfunctional relationships, emotional overeating, risky sexual behavior, intentional unhealthy habits, or any number of other things, we must be mindful that self-destructive acts are designed to kill us on an installment plan. A little here and a little there, and before you know it, you're being rushed to the hospital. At its core self-destructive behavior is an act of self-hate. You must choose to love yourself too much to allow Satan to manipulate you into hurting yourself.

I often tell people if the devil could have killed you, he would have done it by now. The devil may tempt and torment you, but he does not have the power to take your life when you belong to God. In the Book of Job we eavesdrop on a private conversation between God and Satan. Satan's argument was that Job's commitment to God was connected to his material possessions. To prove Satan's theory wrong, God allowed Satan to take Job through hard trials and tribulations. God gave Satan the following instructions: "Behold, all that he has is in your power; only do not lay a hand on his person" (Job 1:12). The trials Job endured at the hand of Satan included the loss of all his possessions, his children, and his relationships, but he did not lose his life because he belonged to God.

Satan and the demonic team designated to torment you will wage war against you to drive you to a place where you will begin to war against yourself. The enemy and all demonic forces desire to get you to a point where you believe God has forsaken you, and in turn their hope is that you will turn your back on God. Turning your back on God leaves you in a mental space that causes you to harm yourself in various ways. Your disconnection leads to your demise, as it causes you to inflict harm upon yourself that will manifest spiritually, mentally, emotionally, and physically.

Let's take a closer look at how this spirit manifested in the man living among the tombs. The spirit tormented the man day and night. Unclean spirits usually don't work nine to five. They are persistent and don't rest. Around the clock every day, this spirit manifested in one capacity or another in the man's life. Before now you may have experienced spiritual attacks and you didn't even realize what was happening. These attacks may have been in the form of unusual exhaustion, far beyond the scope of what your daily activity created. You knew something was awry because "your tired was tired." The attacks may have even presented themselves in other subtle ways, such as difficulty studying or working on the next project. And you may have felt in your spirit that something wasn't right, but you couldn't quite put your finger on it. What you have been dealing with is what I describe as a sleepless spirit. It has been my experience that spiritual attacks threaten your sleep at night and your focus during the day because Satan wants to distract you from your efforts that bring God glory.

Being attacked by spirits that will not sleep is challenging because if the spirit isn't sleeping, the person with the spirit is probably not sleeping either. I would go to bed by myself and wake up to discover a few pillows and all the sheets were off the bed. I realized at that point that I was being attacked in my sleep. Although I was closing my eyes for the night, my spirit was not at rest. I would be tired during the day and couldn't figure out why. I now realize I was under a spiritual attack that was determined to be active 24/7. When Paul wrote in 1 Thessalonians 5:17 to "pray without ceasing," he was offering a powerful word of wisdom. Prayer is what keeps us protected, and if the enemy will attack without ceasing, our prayers should match his level of attack.

When spirits attack you like this, they are attempting to rob you of your productivity. If you are preoccupied with these manifestations around the clock, you are constantly in a state of warfare. This can hinder your focus, and it can attack your physical and mental health. But there is good news. According to a study from the University of Florida in Gainesville and Wayne State University in Detroit, older adults use prayer more than any other alternative health therapy, and 96 percent of study participants used prayer "to specifically cope with stress."[1] Spirituality plays a vital role in maintaining your overall health and well-being; therefore, it is essential that you become aware of the spiritual attacks that come to affect every area of your life.

GUARD AGAINST SPIRITUAL ATTACK

Often our communities of faith have been inept in dealing with spiritual suppression of believers and possession of nonbelievers because we lack the programs, protocols, and power to overcome demonic attack. When these things are in place, we are positioned most effectively to win. For example, by using programs designed to train the community to properly identify what is happening with a person, we gain the upper hand on the enemy's intent to further torment. Rather than respond with chains the way the Gadarenes did, we will respond with change. Our desire to see people free should supersede our temptation to lock down and lock up.

Protocols are in place to de-escalate and to position for deliverance to take place. There were instances in which Jesus, needing to create a more secure and intimate deliverance situation, did not let anyone follow Him except just a few, and other times He asked people to leave the room.

Power is when we activate our authority over the demonic force and cast it out. It is one thing to call it out, and something entirely different to cast it out. When people are possessed, they do not hold the capacity to free themselves. This is where we come in as believers. In Matthew 10:1 "Jesus called his twelve disciples to him and gave them authority to drive out impure spirits and to heal every disease and sickness" (NIV). Part of the reason so many unclean spirits are running rampant is the church's ineptness to do this work. As Spirit-filled believers we possess the authority to cast out demons. You cannot fraudulently use this authority. It won't work. Either you have it, or you don't. We can have all the programs and protocol under the sun, but if we lack power, we will never be able to help ourselves or others become free. By all means, do not attempt to call out what you cannot cast out! Check your power before trying to become an expert exorcist, or you will end up like the seven sons of Sceva in Acts 19.

While attacks are certain to come, you can create a plan of action to guard yourself against the spiritual attacks seeking to seep into every area of your life. The following are steps you can take to help protect yourself from being subdued when attacks arise:

Place prayer on your daily schedule.

Again, 1 Thessalonians 5:17 instructs us to "pray without ceasing." Prayer should be included in your daily schedule. You should never be too busy to pray. The devil is never too busy to attack you, which means you should always remain alert and connected to God through prayer. To have a level of prayer that matches the level of attacks you will encounter, you must include the following strategy in your daily prayer schedule:

- **Eliminate distractions.** Find a quiet place where you can be alone with God. Avoid having your phone near or any device that would cause you to become distracted while you are in a time of one-on-one conversation with God.

- **Increase your time in prayer.** You cannot constantly have a few scattered moments of prayer and expect to have a level of communication with God that matches the level of the enemy's attack on your life. Your increase can be seen in the following manner: in a twenty-four-hour period, if you are awake at least sixteen hours of the day, you should devote at least a tithe, one-tenth, of your awake hours to prayer. This would result in your spending one to two hours per day in prayer and communication with God.

- **Feed your spirit.** In addition to your time in prayer it is essential that you take time to ensure your spirit is filled with the Word of God. You must become equipped with the power of the Scriptures to combat the attacks of the enemy. The Word of God, according to Hebrews 4:12, "is alive and powerful. It is sharper than the sharpest two-edged sword, cutting between soul and spirit, between joint and marrow. It exposes our innermost thoughts and desires" (NLT). The more knowledgeable you are of the Word of God, the more equipped you will be to handle the attacks against you.

Remain connected to communities of faith.

Hebrews 10:25 instructs believers to not forsake "the assembling of ourselves together, as is the manner of some, but exhorting one another, and so much the more as you see the Day approaching." In order for people to not forsake the assembly, the assembly must not forsake the people. In other words, the communities to which struggling people retreat for help cannot ignore them and throw them to the margins. As communities of faith it is our responsibility to create an environment equipped to handle the diverse and unique ways those experiencing struggle show up.

I want to encourage those of you who are under attack to not check out. You cannot live in a silo; you are not an island unto yourself. You are a member of the body of Christ, and your presence is necessary for all parts of the body to operate efficiently. Your connection with the church is also essential when you are under attack. When you are connected to the right people, you have a larger base of power from which you can combat spiritual attacks because, according to Deuteronomy 32:30, we know that one can "chase a thousand," but two joined together can "put ten thousand to flight."

Commit to overall health and wellness.

First Corinthians 6:19 informs us that our bodies are the temple of the Holy Spirit. Therefore we should honor God with our bodies. God needs us to be in optimum health so we will be fit for use in the kingdom. When we do not maintain our physical, mental, and emotional health, we are neglecting our responsibility to be good stewards over our spiritual houses. When your mind, body, and spirit are filled with good things, it will leave little to no room for Satan to take up residence and launch spiritual attacks within you.

Live a focused life and maintain a positive outlook.

Keep your mind on God, and you will be better prepared to guard yourself against the attacks that will come against you. Isaiah 26:3 gives us this assurance: "You will keep him in perfect peace, whose mind is stayed on You, because he trusts in You." When you keep your mind on God and trust Him, you will remain in a state of peace even when chaos attempts to arise around you. Not only must you remain focused, but you must also maintain a positive mindset.

Staying positive will keep you focused on God's ability to keep you. Negative thoughts will open the door for words and actions that are counter to who God is and what He is doing in your life. Negativity is a breeding ground for contempt and bitterness. To ward off spiritual attacks, you must not give any place for the devil in your life.

According to clinical and forensic psychologist Stephen A. Diamond, PhD, bitterness is "a chronic and pervasive state of smoldering resentment, [and it] is one of the most destructive and toxic of human emotions....Bitterness is a prolonged, resentful feeling of disempowered and devalued victimization."[2] Philosopher Friedrich Nietzsche once stated that "nothing on earth consumes a man more quickly than the passion of resentment."[3] Do not allow negativity to be your guide, but develop a positive approach to life and remain focused on the good plans God has for your life (Jer. 29:11). Philippians 4:8 gives us wisdom on how to guide our thoughts in a more positive direction, telling us, "Whatsoever things are true, whatsoever things are honest, whatsoever things are just, whatsoever things are pure, whatsoever things are lovely, whatsoever things are of good report; if there be any virtue, and if there be any praise, think on these things" (KJV).

Each of the previous steps is designed to help you create the structure in your life to have a built-in system of defense against spiritual attacks. Take authority over your life by embracing the strategy to stop the enemy from robbing of you of your sleep, sanity, and success another day.

FROM THE MOUNTAINTOP TO THE TOMBS

There is another aspect of this manifestation we must consider. The spirit took the man up to the mountain and back to the tombs. This suggests there is an intentional effort to take the man between two extremes and to do it often. Quite frequently ministry leaders experience these highs and lows, and we find ourselves living between two extremes. We are on the mountain on Sunday and Wednesday but go home and spend time in the tombs through the remainder of the week.

The prophet Elijah provides us with a biblical example of a person who found himself living between these two extremes. The Bible tells us Elijah came to a point in his life where he was depressed and wanted to throw in the towel. In 1 Kings 18 Elijah saw God literally send fire from heaven during a showdown on Mount Carmel that left 450 prophets of Baal dead and turned the Israelites back to the one true God. But when the wicked queen Jezebel threatened to kill him just as he had killed her prophets, Elijah fled for his life.

Elijah ran to the wilderness, where God miraculously provided food that sustained him for forty days and forty nights as he traveled to Horeb. But when Elijah arrived in Horeb, which is referred to as the mountain of God, he went into a cave, a dark and damp place, to spend the night. Elijah's confrontation with the prophets of Baal on Mount Carmel is considered one of the greatest miracles recorded in the Old Testament. But just a few verses after this incredible display of God's power Elijah had become so despondent that he sought refuge in a cave.

God had to pull him out of that state by asking, "What are you doing here, Elijah?" (1 Kings 19:13). This question had less to do with Elijah's physical location and more to do with Elijah's emotional well-being and spiritual location. God, who is omniscient, knew where Elijah was and what was going on with him, but He needed Elijah to acknowledge his current emotional state so he could begin the process of dealing with his depression. Elijah's response is recorded in verse 14: "And he said, I have been very jealous for the LORD God of hosts: because the children of Israel have forsaken thy covenant, thrown down thine altars, and slain thy prophets with the sword; and I, even I only, am left; and they seek my life, to take it away" (KJV).

Elijah became overwhelmed after fighting a great spiritual battle and then finding himself running from the enemies of God, which led him into a cave. Elijah felt forsaken by God, so he let his emotions get the best of him, which became the entryway for depression to set in. At this point he had gone from a mountain experience just days earlier to a dark cave, wanting to give up. But a one-on-one encounter with the Lord helped him see things in a new light and come out of the dark place the cave represented. The Lord came to Elijah in a still, small voice to minister to him, and after some more dialogue the Lord told Elijah there were seven thousand other prophets in Israel who had not bowed their knees to Baal. There is something comforting in knowing that you are not the only one going through a particular situation. Elijah then had a new perspective and was able to continue his assignment. He also found Elisha, the one who would serve him until his earthly assignment was completed.

Elijah needed a new perspective on his life because he had been in the situation so long that his focus had settled upon what was happening to him, which made it difficult for him to see the good God was doing through him. Elijah was stuck in the tombs of his trials and tribulation because he felt helpless. But it is in these times that God helps us, often with the gift of hope and camaraderie. Upon hearing there were thousands of others in Israel who were still standing for the righteousness of God, Elijah realized he was not in the experience by himself.

The persistent journey from the tomb to the mountaintop and back again is all too real for so many people. I experienced these extremes when my first wife was diagnosed with cancer. The attack we endured caused us to feel constantly conflicted. Pastoring a great church where thousands gathered on the weekend became the mountain. Going home to a private struggle with her sickness became the tombs. I would go up to the mountain and preach the Word and then go down to the tombs and wrestle in my brokenness, questioning God and struggling in my faith. It was up to the mountain to watch others get healed and back to the tombs to wonder if it was going to happen for us. As I've served God's people for over twenty-five years, I've learned that quite a few people live this reality every single day. These are the people smiling and telling you they are living their best life while simultaneously experiencing a private attack that threatens to unravel their confidence in what they proclaim to be true.

When you are a leader, it's difficult to go through seasons like this because people expect you to have it all together. People don't expect you to go through the lows of life because they often see you inspiring them to live in the high places. Leaders are also misunderstood because people assume that since leaders can stand strong as they minister under the anointing, they are that strong when dealing with everyday life situations. It must be said that leaders hurt too. Leaders bleed too. However, far too often leaders feel forced to lead while they bleed, and there is hardly anyone spiritually skilled enough to help change a leader's bandages without exposing his or her wounds to deeper infection. Therefore leaders wind up becoming wounded healers who provide urgent care services to countless others while lacking the very care they need for themselves.

This model of leadership, with the leader receiving little to no care, is based on a false perception that leaders have it all together. However, data collected from numerous pastors and church leaders is raising awareness to the fact that leaders don't necessarily have it all together. A 2016 study of over eight thousand ministers conducted by the Francis A. Schaeffer Institute of Church Leadership Development noted the following regarding church leaders:

- "57% can't pay their bills.

- 54% are overworked and 43% are overstressed.

- 53% feel seminary had not properly prepared them for the task.

- 35% battle depression.

- 26% are overly fatigued.

- 28% are spiritually undernourished and 9% are burnt-out.

- 23% are…distant to their families.

- 18% work more than 70 hours a week and face unreasonable challenges.…

- 65% of pastors feel their family is in a 'glass house' and fear they are not good enough to meet expectations.…

- 52% of pastors feel they are overworked and can't meet their church's unrealistic expectations.…

- 58% of pastors feel they do not have any good true friends.…

- 34% of pastors battle discouragement on a regular basis.…

- 27% of pastors stated they have no one to turn to if they are facing a crisis."[4]

I share these statistics to let you know that if you are a leader, you are not alone in the struggles you face on a daily basis. This myth that leaders retain a special layer of strength and capacity to do the impossible must be debunked among those who support leaders and among leaders themselves. Many of us have been trained to take on unreasonable expectations of leadership. Due to false perceptions we harbor of our own responsibility and capacity to lead, we fall victim to the consequences of our own decisions.

It is time for our church communities to discontinue overspiritualizing the issues that often drive leaders into the tombs. If leaders do not receive help when they experience these tomb-like situations, then devastating consequences will follow. This has become more evident over the past few years with the increase of suicide among pastors, which has sent shock waves through the Christian community. Some of the suicides are a result of the effects of mental illness. A 2016 Gospel Coalition article titled "Why Pastors Are Committing Suicide" reported that about 23 percent of pastors say they have experienced some type of mental illness. Additionally, according to LifeWay research, 12 percent of pastors have been diagnosed with a mental health condition.[5]

The Gospel Coalition article shares an assessment by Chuck Hannaford, "a clinical psychologist who consults for the Southern Baptist Convention." He "believes the rate of pastor suicides has increased during his 30 years of practice," and sadly, based on his research, he expects the number to rise. He said, "Being a pastor is a dangerous job.... Especially in certain evangelical circles, where you have more of a fundamentalist orientation theologically, you find pastors who will reduce their depression or their negative thought processes to strictly spiritual problems."[6]

This battle cannot be considered a strictly spiritual issue that is fought only with spiritual methods. We must find balance when manifestation occurs. You must continue to pray, fast, and have faith that God will deliver you from the attacks unclean spirits lodge against you, but you must understand that clinical methods must also be used. Over time the unclean spirits that attack you have long-term effects on your mind and body that call for you to engage in more than spiritual warfare. There is often also a need for clinical counseling and therapy to help you cope with the realities you face daily. Help is available to you. Do not remain in this without getting help. If you find yourself in a predicament where you feel like giving up, seek help immediately, whether day or night. If you or someone you know is contemplating suicide, please call the National Suicide Prevention Lifeline at 1-800-273-8255 or visit SuicidePreventionLifeline.org.

Numerous times I've shared with leaders in private our common struggles in dealing with these types of attacks. Some mountains are higher than others. Whatever size your mountain, it has its own complexities. The more God does in your life, the greater your exposure. And when you are operating at certain altitudes, the fewer people there are who can truly comprehend your struggle. When you are an authentic person, it's difficult when the attacks force you to be disingenuous while you are on the mountain. Perhaps this has contributed to the high rate of depression and suicide among kingdom leaders.

There are times when you just want to cry out and say, "I'm tired" or "I'm hurting." But you press on and reserve your complaints until you return to the tombs, where nobody hears you among the dead. I need to tell you that it's OK not to be OK. It's OK to be honest about your weakness and to go before God not as a spiritual superhero but as a broken servant in need of redemption. Paul received a response from Christ when he was in crisis that speaks to us today: "And he said unto me, My grace is sufficient for thee: for my strength is made perfect in weakness. Most gladly therefore will I rather glory in my infirmities, that the power of Christ may rest upon me" (2 Cor. 12:9, kjv).

I tell young people all the time to make sure they are patient as they pursue the mountains in life because they will need a certain level of preparedness when they get there. I remember my first time going to New York. I'm from Louisiana, so it was a huge learning curve for this Southerner. I will always remember my first subway ride and how God spoke to me. I had to go down the steps to catch the subway. While I was enjoying the ride, God told me there were people above me who were unaware of my presence. Though I was underground and unnoticed, I was still moving. God reminded me that in life He often allows us to have seasons in the subway, where we can work through certain struggles and make mistakes before He elevates us to street level. If you are in the subway in your ministry or career, don't despise it; embrace it. There is a grace you can experience only at that level that may not be as obvious among people when you reach your next level.

TOSSED BETWEEN TWO EXTREMES

If you find yourself vacillating between the mountain and the tombs, it is simply a manifestation of the spiritual warfare you are experiencing. In full transparency, during my time between these two extremes I found myself smiling on the mountain and crying in the tombs. The mountain is where we put on our game face. It's where we encounter the expectations of others. It's the place where we have to be strong for everyone else, so we put our issues on the back burner and do the best we can to maintain our image. When you experience this level of attack, you just do what you have to do to hold it together.

Although you are smiling externally on the mountain, you are broken internally. If the people around you had any idea how fragile you were, it would have huge implications. I remember going up to the mountain to preach and then down to the tombs, sitting in a room injecting Phenergan into an IV line so my late wife could manage her nausea. I was going up to the mountain to encourage everybody else and then down to the tombs needing encouragement myself. It would have been better to just remain at one location and develop the capacity to function there; however, this spirit specializes in thrusting you between the two. As soon as you develop a survival mechanism that works on the mountain, you are whisked back to the tombs and vice versa. Unless you've experienced this, it's hard to understand.

By now you should see a pattern. The manifestation is not random; it's methodical. It is designed to bring you to a place of exhaustion so you are unable to function or fight. It takes you to these extremes to exploit your pain so you will do what the man in Mark 5 did. The Scripture says he was crying out and cutting himself. We do the same thing, but we tend to cry out only in the tombs. On the mountain we usually present an image that we have it together and wait until we return to the tombs to cry. The irony is that so often we don't cry on the mountain when we are near those who can hear and help, but we do cry in the tombs where we are struggling alone, surrounded by others dealing with the same issues. The enemy's ultimate goal is to exhaust us with this sort of roaming—back and forth, up and down, and getting nowhere.

The man among the tombs also began cutting himself. Though there are real cases where cutting happens today, this man's behavior reveals a broader issue among those who experience spiritual warfare. Though you may not physically cut yourself, it is possible to cause self-inflicted wounds in your life. Some people do cut themselves, leaving marks to remind them of their failures. They mark themselves with labels, slash opportunities with negligence and irresponsibility, sever relationships with lies and deceit, and butcher their purpose through rebellion. Often the decisions we make as a result of our unreconciled pain cause us to cut ourselves. There is no pleasure in cutting yourself, but when you are under spiritual attack, you are emotionally and physically removed from the effects of the cutting. In other words, the internal torment dulls the external trauma. This allows us to continue the cutting without realizing the impact it is having on our lives.

Often others can see us bleeding before we do. People who care about us will come and share with us their observations concerning what we are doing to ourselves, yet we will shut them out because we have a different interpretation than they do. When you are cutting yourself, you never think it's as bad as others say it is. This is how the unclean spirit causes us to justify the cutting: "The relationship is not that bad." "I'm not that drunk." "I'm not that high." "He didn't hit me that hard." "I took only one hit of cocaine."

These are just some of the justifications we use to downplay the impact of the wounds we create in our own lives.

The manifestation of spiritual attack is always to bring embarrassment and shame to your life. The enemy wants to exploit your pain and use your most vulnerable moments to showcase his strength behind the scenes. Satan wants you to do the dirty work while he manipulates the moment. If you succumb and wound yourself, your pain is further enhanced. So many people are dealing with this level of manifestation. If you are experiencing this and feelings of guilt and shame have overwhelmed you, there is hope. The very moment Jesus showed up in Gadara, the man's manifestations ceased, and his attention was shifted away from his pain to what is possible in Christ. Things happen when Jesus shows up! He has come to meet you in your pain and deliver you to your promise.

ROOT WORK

1. What type of hurts have you experienced in your past?

2. Have any of your hurts been self-inflicted?

3. Are you being robbed of your productivity due to spiritual attacks? If yes, in what areas have you experienced loss?

4. Does your role or status cause you to forfeit seeking help when you are under attack? If yes, write down at least three reasons your role is a hindrance to your seeking help.

5. What is your coping mechanism when you feel yourself going between the two extremes of the mountain and the tombs?

CHAPTER 6

Manipulation:
This Is Nonnegotiable

WHEN JESUS SHOWED up in Mark 5, the Scriptures say the unclean spirit initiated the man's interaction with Jesus: "But when he saw Jesus afar off, he ran and worshipped him, and cried with a loud voice, and said, What have I to do with thee, Jesus, thou Son of the most high God? I adjure thee by God, that thou torment me not" (vv. 6–7, KJV). If there is one thing you should know when dealing with demonic spirits, it is that they will attempt to manipulate moments. They also will try negotiating in an attempt to suffer as little loss as possible.

When you are experiencing warfare, you have to draw a line in the sand and refuse to negotiate with demons. Unclean spirits never operate from a place of truth. This is why negotiation is not possible. There can never be any fair negotiation between you and an unclean spirit because the enemy attempts to trick your mind. For this reason 1 Peter 5:8 instructs us to "be sober, be vigilant; because your adversary the devil walks about like a roaring lion, seeking whom he may devour."

When your mind is made unstable because of the

lies demonic spirits tell, they can manipulate you into believing that the way you are living is the way you should be living. They will also attempt to convince you that contact with Jesus will only torment you. This may sound ridiculous to someone who understands the power of Jesus to heal, deliver, and set you free; however, this is not the case for a person who has been bound mentally, physically, and spiritually by unclean spirits perhaps for years. The unclean spirits have become the individual's master, and experiencing torment has become the person's norm. Those needing deliverance don't really fear Jesus; the evil spirits' fear of Jesus is being projected onto them. The unclean spirits do not want to leave, and these spirits are keenly aware that contact with Jesus will mark the beginning of the end of their assault on the person.

This is why we see the man under the influence of the unclean spirits react so extravagantly to Jesus. The demons were hoping Jesus would not evict them from their place of residence. The unclean spirits wanted to keep the man in such a confused state that he would see someone who could bring him deliverance as the enemy. You may know people in this mental and emotional state, people who have found solace in their torment and lash out at the very people who can help them out of that dark place.

For example, a person struggling with a substance abuse issue may see the spouse who is trying to help as someone who wants only to bring her more hurt. The person sees her spouse's suggestion to go to counseling or rehab as a means of torment. Or a teenager who is hanging out with the wrong crowd and becoming involved in illegal activity that is putting him on a sure path to jail or the grave may see the parent who is trying to help as enemy number one. Whatever the situation, the person who is being manipulated by the destructive spirits cannot see the true cause of her torment as a demonic spirit and not the people assigned to lead her to healing. This level of deception can happen only when manipulating spirits have complete access to a person's mind, body, and spirit. In this state the person rejects deliverance ministry because of demonic manipulation.

Once manipulation occurs, it becomes difficult for the person to discern what God desires for his life. This is why Paul wrote in Romans 12:1–2, "I beseech you therefore, brethren, by the mercies of God, that you present your bodies a living sacrifice, holy, acceptable to God, which is your reasonable service. And do not be conformed to this world, but be transformed by the renewing of your mind, that you may prove what is that good and acceptable and perfect will of God." When we renew our minds, we become committed to studying God's Word, and we seek God's will for our lives through prayer. The combination of these two allows us to think differently than we've always thought. This causes us to expand our level of expectations about what we desire out of life and to be clear about what we do not.

It is interesting that the first thing the unclean spirit did when it saw Jesus was to run and worship Him. This form of worship is suspect because demons have a limited capacity to worship, as their whole idea of worship is perverted. They seek not to worship but to be worshipped. Lucifer was thrown out of heaven because he had grown intolerant of all the worship going to God. Isaiah records what happened:

> How you are fallen from heaven, O Lucifer, son of the morning! How you are cut down to the ground, you who weakened the nations! For you have said in your heart: "I will ascend into heaven, I will exalt my throne above the stars of God; I will also sit on the mount of the congregation on the farthest sides of the north; I will ascend above the heights of the clouds, I will be like the Most High." Yet you shall be brought down to Sheol, to the lowest depths of the Pit. Those who see you will gaze at you, and consider you, saying: "Is this the man who made the earth tremble, who shook kingdoms, who made the world as a wilderness and destroyed its cities, who did not open the house of his prisoners?"
>
> —ISAIAH 14:12–17

As a consequence he was cast out, and he and his demons despise worship of God because they don't want to worship Him in truth. You can worship only from a place of truth. The Scripture says in John 4:24, "God is Spirit, and those who worship Him must worship in spirit and truth." How can the father of lies worship in truth? So this expression of worship was offered as a form of manipulation. Disingenuous worship seeks to gain an advantage. It seeks to push an agenda by hiding behind theological jargon and expressions. Paul said in 2 Corinthians 11:14 that "Satan himself transforms himself into an angel of light." The devil seeks to imitate spiritual things to appear harmless.

To worship, you have to declare that Jesus is Lord. That's something Satan cannot do because it would be an open acknowledgment of truth. The devil doesn't operate in truth. He operates in lies, schemes, and pure manipulation. When you are under the influence of unclean spirits and experiencing demonic attack, you have to be mindful that your worship must remain authentic. You cannot allow yourself to engage in what I call recreational religion.

This is when we appear to be engaged through a variety of demonstrative religious expressions and acts that have nothing to do with God. I've been in church all my life, and I have discovered that everything people interpret as the move of the Spirit is not always of God. I believe this happens because unclean spirits need an audience to feed them. They need attention and will do a lot to get it. The fact that the spirit ran to Jesus suggests it wanted to be the center of attention. God is not interested in sharing His glory with an unclean spirit. God said, "I am the LORD, that is My name; and My glory I will not give to another, nor My praise to carved images" (Isa. 42:8).

When people are under demonic attack, Satan manipulates them into acts of overspiritualization. These hyperspiritual acts are attempts to deflect attention from the deeper issues happening in a person's life. There is a thin line between authentic charismatic expressions of worship and demonic manipulation portraying worship. It's manipulation when there is no change in the person's life. Worship transforms your spirit; therefore, when true worship occurs, a transformation and a transfer take place. The transformation is visible in your posture after the worship is over because your walk is different due to your mind being aligned with the thoughts of God.

The transfer that takes place is also a unique occurrence because the weights you had when you entered worship will no longer be with you when your time of worship ends. God needs you to bring all the things that have had you burdened and weighed down to Him and leave them at the altar of worship. This does not have to be a physical altar, but wherever worship occurs will become your place of worship. In our modern-day worship services we have become fixated on our churches as places of worship. However, the Old Testament accounts remind us that wherever God showed up became a place of worship, and the people built an altar there as a reminder. Your home, your car, and even the bathroom on your job can become your place of worship or your altar when you seek to worship God in the spirit of truth.

Manipulating spirits specialize in worshipping worship rather than worshipping God. All of us have heard people say, "We had a great church service today." Yet we know the same people's lives are still in disarray because of the limitation of their acts of worship. Unclean spirits are content with producing churchy people who lack character. We've all seen people like this. They have a tendency to walk with an air of spiritual elitism. They often make us feel they are on another level and that they have a connection with God the rest of us mere mortals could only dream about.

FINDING AND MAINTAINING BALANCE

The more I see this in the body of Christ, the more I am convinced this hyperspiritualism is a cover-up for dysfunction. I remember telling members of my congregation who were at church seven days a week for services or meetings to go home. The ancient philosopher Plato once wrote, "The part can never be well unless the whole is well."[1] You can't take care of one part of you and neglect the other parts of you. You can't focus solely on your spiritual well-being and neglect your physical and emotional well-being.

There is no way your home can be healthy if you are spending the entire week away from it. You need balance in your life because without it you give space for further dysfunction to enter your life. Balance is a key component for a successful life. Having a healthy work-life balance is essential to getting your life in order. Gaining and maintaining balance keeps you from being so depleted that you are too tired to fight off demonic attacks. Having balance puts you on a path toward living a rewarding life. The following are some methods for achieving balance in your life.

- **Schedule downtime.** When you are busy, downtime does not simply happen; it must be created. Building time for rest, relaxing activities, and other things necessary for self-care must be added to your daily routine. Remember: a little relaxation goes a long way. As little as fifteen minutes of relaxation during the course of the day can help recharge your batteries.

- **Remove distractions and unnecessary activities.** This includes removing people who tend to distract in addition to unnecessary activities that distract from established goals.

- **Set aside quality time for family and friends.** Relationships matter. Setting aside quality time without outside distractions helps to foster and produce healthy relationships. Take the time to get to know the people with whom you are in relationship.

- **Remember to enjoy life and have fun.** Learn how to laugh, joke, play, and have fun. Take time to explore the world and expand your awareness. Do something interesting; take a class in something that interests you; learn a new language. Learn how to treat yourself and enjoy your life.

Religion is often used as an escape route by people who don't want to address the deeper issues in their lives. God is not interested in worship that doesn't transform us. When we are delivered, there is continuity in our worship and our lifestyle. Real worship is a result of a relationship with God where you are comfortable being vulnerable and transparent before Him. Real worship removes pretentiousness and challenges us to live in truth before God and man.

According to a 2017 Vanderbilt University study, men and women between the ages of forty and sixty-five "who attend church or other houses of worship reduce their risk for mortality by 55 percent. 'Our findings support the overall hypothesis that increased religiosity—as determined by attendance at worship services—is associated with less stress and enhanced longevity,'" said social and behavioral scientist Marino Bruce, PhD. "We've found that being in a place where you can flex those spiritual muscles is actually beneficial for your health."[2] I have discovered that attending church and enjoying fellowship among other believers is incredibly beneficial. Attending worship allows you to receive a word that counters the numerous negative things the enemy has spoken in your life. Knowing what God says about your life and is saying to you right now will put you in a better posture and place. There is also a great deal of encouragement you can receive in knowing firsthand you are not alone in your struggles.

BE WHO YOU ARE

After the unclean spirit fell down before Jesus, it immediately questioned the reason for the encounter. The spirit presented itself with the pronoun *I,* which was another attempt at manipulation. We will discover later that "I" was actually "we." Not only do unclean spirits attempt to hide their intentions, but they also seek to hide their identities. In writing about the "Basics of Identity," Shahram Heshmat, PhD, stated that "identity is concerned largely with the question: 'Who are you?'" It relates to the "values that dictate the choices we make."[3]

Yet Heshmat notes that "few people choose their identities. Instead, they simply internalize the values of their parents or the dominant cultures.…Sadly, these values may not be aligned with one's authentic self and create unfulfilling life. In contrast, fulfilled people are able to live a life true to their values and pursue meaningful goals. Lack of a coherent sense of identity will lead to uncertainty about what one wants to do in life."[4]

If the spirit hides its identity, it also seeks to hide the identity of the person it attacks. This is why so often people present their best surface self to prevent discovery of the deeper struggles they've camouflaged for years.

ANOINTING AND AUTHORITY

One of the things you will discover about demonic spirits is that they recognize the anointing and the authority upon your life. (I will discuss your authority in Christ in the next chapter.) The spirit that tormented the man in the tombs pleaded with Jesus not to torment it. Although the spirit was aggressive and violent, it acknowledged an authority greater than itself. Paul wrote in Philippians 2:10–11, "At the name of Jesus every knee should bow, of those in heaven, and of those on earth, and of those under the earth, and that every tongue should confess that Jesus Christ is Lord, to the glory of God the Father."

I remember going to the store with my friends when I was a young kid. We would get off the bus and take the journey every day down Alma Street. Without fail we would be harassed by Mr. Johnson's dog. It would bark and growl at us, and we could tell it was a big, ferocious dog. We knew the exact point to take off running. One day I got tired of running and decided to send my friends ahead to the store. I went to Mr. Johnson's house and shared with him that we were just kids trying to go to the store and that his dog was terrorizing the neighborhood. I respectfully asked him to make it stop. Mr. Johnson shared something with me I never shall forget. The next day when we got off the bus and turned down Alma Street, everyone took off running except me. When I finally arrived at the store, my friends were bewildered at my recent development of bravery and asked me why I didn't run from the dog.

I told them that I had spoken to the dog's owner and he informed me of something important. Although his dog was big and had large teeth, he assured me that he kept him on a leash. As a consequence the dog could only go so far. All those times we had walked by Mr. Johnson's house, we only saw the dog. We were so intimidated by his size and aggressive barking that we never even noticed the leash. You may be experiencing fear from the enemy that consistently attempts to intimidate you. God is reminding you today that the devil is on a leash and can only go so far. Can you imagine where your life would be if God did not have the devil on a leash?

Once the unclean spirit realizes it is in the presence of a much greater authority, it attempts to negotiate. What Jesus teaches us is that there is no place for negotiation. He immediately speaks to the spirit and tells it to come out of the man. When you are dealing with demons, you have to walk in uncompromising authority. So often we find ourselves making compromises to accommodate the demons while at the same time extending the havoc they have brought in our lives. Maybe you are in a situation where demons are attempting to negotiate with you concerning their tenure in your life. Maybe it's a toxic relationship with a person who continues to pursue another chance with you. Perhaps it's a private struggle or addiction that is seeking one more time to engage your life. There comes a point in time in your life when you must draw a line in the sand. It will serve as the demarcation line the devil can no longer cross. You have to come to a point where you will declare enough is enough. If you continue to allow demons of the past to infiltrate your present life, you will carry those demons into your future, and you will continue to live a life of perpetual pain.

Have you ever taken a close look at the story of Jonah on the ship during the storm? It is a fact that Jonah was operating with a spirit of disobedience, and that spirit brought a storm into the lives of everyone connected to him. Have you noticed that when people are out of the will of God, they attract storms in their lives and those storms affect the lives of others? Much of the chaos you may be experiencing in certain relationships could be the result of someone out of the will of God. These storms are indiscriminate. More importantly they are fueled by willful disobedience. I've had seasons of my life that were so peaceful, but when certain people arrived, things became turbulent. This is tough.

You didn't ask for this storm, yet it has been imposed upon you by someone else's decisions.

Jonah was fleeing the call of God and boarded a ship to Tarshish. But because he was in disobedience, God sent a storm so strong it threatened to destroy the ship. When the crew questioned Jonah, they discovered the cause of their peril. Jonah told them of his disobedience and informed them that if they would throw him overboard, the storm would stop and their lives would be saved. Jonah acknowledged that he was the problem.

What do you do when your problem tells you it's the problem? Maybe someone in your life is acting out in ways that are unhealthy and unproductive. He may be telling you he is the problem. When someone refuses to come home when she is supposed to, she could be saying she is the problem. When a person's life puts everything and everyone around him in jeopardy, it could be an indication that he is telling you he is the problem.

Something interesting occurred in Jonah's story. After he told the ship's crew to throw him overboard because the storm was his fault and that once they did, the sea would become calm, the sailors "did their best to row back to land. But they could not, for the sea grew even wilder than before" (Jon. 1:13, NIV). Have there been times in your life when it was clear you needed to let something go, but you continued trying to make the situation work? This is called the messiah complex. You think it's your personal responsibility to save someone who doesn't want to be saved.

These men put everything they had worked for in jeopardy trying to negotiate with something that was determined to destroy them. I've seen people spend valuable years of their lives attempting to continue rowing with something that was destined to fail. When you do this, you waste precious moments that you will never recover. How long will you row before you realize the negative impact this is having on your life? When I think of the days, months, and years I wasted trying to make certain things work that were inevitably going to fail, a variety of emotions begin to arise. These seasons will leave you battered and bitter and full of unmet expectations.

My word to you today is to stop the madness. I know you are a good person, but you can't allow the enemy to manipulate your heartstrings and bring about your demise. You can't continue to tolerate and accommodate things that are set on destroying you. This kind of demonic manipulation is determined to exploit your good intentions. The people on the ship with Jonah were threatened by the storm, but that was not the source. The source of their struggle was Jonah's disobedience to God. All struggles have a source, and it is often Satan behind the scenes pulling the strings.

I would be one of the people who didn't want to throw Jonah off the boat. What I have had to realize is that God has made provisions for the Jonahs who come into my life. The Jonahs belong to God, not to me. This may be a wonderful opportunity for you to do what I've learned to do in these types of situations. I've learned to release my Jonahs into their destinies. If you keep Jonah on your ship, neither of you will make it to your destination. You could potentially be hindering your Jonah from the will of God for his life. The poet Maya Angelou once said, "When people show you who they are, believe them the first time."[5]

If you are serious about ending this struggle in your life, you have to declare that you are not willing to negotiate with unclean spirits. You have to serve them notice that you will no longer be under their control. There can be no back and forth with demons. You have to stand strong in your convictions. You have to walk in the authority God has given you. There is no place for timidity when you are experiencing warfare.

When you walk in authority, you make concrete decisions about moving on with your life and never looking back. You do as Paul proclaimed in Philippians 3:13–14: "Brethren, I count not myself to have apprehended: but this one thing I do, forgetting those things which are behind, and reaching forth unto those things which are before, I press toward the mark for the prize of the high calling of God in Christ Jesus" (KJV).

ROOT WORK

1. Has there been an instance in your life when an unclean spirit has tried to negotiate with you? If so, please explain how you responded.

2. How do you avoid recreational religion and get to an authentic place of worship?

3. What methods do you utilize to achieve balance in your life?

4. How would you describe yourself if you were asked, "Who are you?"

5. Are you ready to end the struggles in your life? If so, list three things you can do now to start the process.

CHAPTER 7

Confrontation:
This Has to Happen

I N LIFE THERE will always be moments when you have to make decisions that have lasting implications. These are moments when the rubber meets the road. I believe that nothing in life just happens. There are no casual encounters. I wrote a book titled *No Opportunity Wasted: The Art of Execution* in which I explained the importance of moving in your moment. Either you maximize the moment or you miss it. Moments have long-term implications, and if you are apathetic or hesitate, you can run the risk of disrupting the divine plan of God for your life. When the opportunity presents itself, you must move!

The unclean spirit was not expecting Jesus. No appointment was made, but when this encounter occurred, the spirit was very aware that Jesus would not miss this moment of confrontation. After this unclean spirit cried out to Jesus in a blatant attempt to manipulate Him, Jesus confronted it. This confrontation was not some random, knee-jerk reaction; rather, it was intentional and authoritative. Mark 5:8 says, "For He said to him, 'Come out of the man, unclean spirit!'" Jesus served this unclean spirit notice that its tenure had come to an end. Even if it does not seem like the most convenient time, when you are determined to see a change and end the struggle in your life, you will do what you have to do.

Some people avoid confrontation, and they do this for a variety of reasons, including fear that things won't change or a belief that it will make the person angry or ruin the relationship. Some people simply believe confrontation is bad, but in reality confrontation is healthy because it allows you to get to the heart of the issue.

One of the main reasons people avoid confrontation is the fear that the person will become angry and defensive. When you are confronting unclean spirits, they may seek to attack you in retaliation for pointing out the truth about the situation. After all, when you confront a demon, you do so with the intent of declaring its tenure has come to an end. You are rejecting its lies and declaring God's Word, and it should be no surprise that would upset it. Yet avoiding confrontation regarding spiritual attacks allows space for these unclean spirits to continue to wreak havoc on your life and in the lives of the people around you. So no matter how the enemy may resist you, confrontation is critical for deliverance.

Elijah's confrontation with Ahab, king of Israel, is an example of the challenges that come with calling out the unclean spirits at work against the people of God. In 1 Kings 19 the Scriptures state that Jezebel, the wife of King Ahab, sent death threats to Elijah when she found out he had executed the prophets of the idol god Baal on Mount Carmel. All those prophets held an allegiance to Jezebel, and she was so angered by Elijah's action, she sent word that she would have him killed by the next day. Yet Jezebel was unable to kill Elijah because he was protected by God.

The confrontation of evil spirits will not come without heightened warfare because the spirits at work know they are condemned to hell, and they want to operate on the earth as long as possible. But their operation must be stopped. This is why you can't let threats from demonic spirits stop you. They have no power over you. When Elijah understood the evil spirit working through Jezebel had no real power over him, he continued to do the work of the Lord by confronting the demonic activity of Ahab and those connected to him.

Toward the end of Ahab's life he was involved in the murder of a man named Naboth. First Kings 21 tells us that Ahab had desired to purchase a vineyard that Naboth owned. When Ahab requested to purchase the land, Naboth refused to sell it to him. Ahab was so upset about being denied the purchase of the land, he would not eat. His wife, Jezebel, found Ahab in this state of depression and asked him what was wrong. He explained what had occurred between him and Naboth, and Jezebel jumped into action. To secure the vineyard her husband desired, Jezebel had Naboth murdered. After Ahab learned that Naboth was dead, he got up and went down to take possession of the long-desired vineyard.

As a result of Jezebel and Ahab's treacherous act the Lord spoke the following words to the prophet Elijah: "Arise, go down to meet Ahab king of Israel, who lives in Samaria. There he is, in the vineyard of Naboth, where he has gone down to take possession of it. You shall speak to him, saying, 'Thus says the LORD: "Have you murdered and also taken possession?"' And you shall speak to him, saying, 'Thus says the Lord: "In the place where dogs licked the blood of Naboth, dogs shall lick your blood, even yours"'" (1 Kings 21:18–19). Elijah had to confront the spirits at work in Jezebel and Ahab to see an end to their reign of terror in Israel.

If real change is going to take place in your life concerning the things you hold dear, confrontation must occur. Perhaps you are like me and you are not a confrontational person. I try to avoid conflict at all cost. I'm just wired that way. When it comes to spiritual warfare, you have to be confrontational. It comes with the territory. This is why it is not done in the flesh but in the Spirit. This spirit had spent years tormenting the man in Mark 5. Without confrontation it would continue to wreak havoc on him and his community.

Yet there can be no confrontation where there is no conviction. If a person is not truly convicted concerning a thing, he will never make the changes necessary to experience the breakthrough he so desperately needs. Confrontation birthed out of conviction refuses to settle and struggle another day.

This message is not for the faint of heart. This is the reality of spiritual warfare.

TOOLS FOR WARFARE

When you are confronting demons, it is important that you address the demons directly. Although everyone in the community saw the man, Jesus spoke directly to the source of the man's troubles. People often want to tiptoe around the real problem. You're not just a little sad; you're not having trouble controlling your spending just because you lack discipline.

Ephesians 6:12 tells us that "we wrestle not against flesh and blood, but against principalities, against powers, against the rulers of the darkness of this world, against spiritual wickedness in high places" (KJV). Spiritual warfare is not tangible and is not fought physically. Therefore you must learn how to go behind the curtain, like Toto did in *The Wizard of Oz*, and find out what spirit is calling strategic plays upon your life.

You have the power to pull down the invisible stronghold that is presenting arguments and rising up against you, but you must use the right tools.

> Therefore take up the whole armor of God, that you may be able to withstand in the evil day, and having done all, to stand. Stand therefore, having girded your waist with truth, having put on the breastplate of righteousness, and having shod your feet with the preparation of the gospel of peace; above all, taking the shield of faith with which you will be able to quench all the fiery darts of the wicked one. And take the helmet of salvation, and the sword of the Spirit, which is the word of God.
>
> —EPHESIANS 6:13–17

This passage provides a list of tools you will need for the spiritual warfare you will encounter. I want to look at each one.

- **The girdle of truth:** This represents your ability to clearly understand God's Word. Having clarity concerning God's Word is essential as you approach a spiritual battle. The enemy will attempt to twist the truth. Your knowledge of the Word allows you to stand strong in the face of every satanic lie. John 8:32 declares, "And you shall know the truth, and the truth shall make you free."

- **The breastplate of righteousness:** This covering piece demonstrates your obedience to God and His Word. Satan will attempt to cause you to disobey God's Word. He will taunt and challenge the Word that has been sown in your life. You cannot just know the Word, but you also must live out the Word. Psalm 119:11 declares, "Thy word have I hid in mine heart, that I might not sin against thee" (KJV).

- **Feet shod with the preparation of the gospel of peace:** Those who are called to proclaim the Word of God must be faithful in their ministry. It is always the agenda of the enemy to remove you from your place of purpose. Your faithfulness is tied to your faith. Your faith is tied to the Word of God. Isaiah 52:7 declares, "How beautiful upon the mountains are the feet of him who brings good news, who proclaims peace, who brings glad tidings of good things, who proclaims salvation, who says to Zion, "Your God reigns!"

- **The shield of faith:** This is meant to cover your entire body. The shield grows as your faith grows. Therefore you must hear the Word of God to increase your shield of faith. Romans 10:17 declares, "So then faith comes by hearing, and hearing by the word of God."

- **The helmet of salvation:** The helmet of salvation serves as head gear, protecting your mind and thoughts, allowing you to maintain a dominion mindset. The enemy will attempt to create chaos in your mind. He knows if your mind is unstable, everything else will be. Isaiah 26:3 says, "Thou wilt keep him in perfect peace, whose mind is stayed on thee: because he trusteth in thee" (KJV). And Philippians 4:8 declares, "Finally, brethren, whatever things are true, whatever things are noble, whatever things are just, whatever things are pure, whatever things are lovely, whatever things are of good report, if there is any virtue and if there is anything praiseworthy—meditate on these things."

- **The sword of the Spirit, which is the Word of God:** This shows you how to use the Word of God offensively. The other pieces of armor are defensive gear, but the Word of God allows you to walk in authority in the face of every attack. When you use the sword of the Spirit, you determine the rules of engagement with the enemy. Hebrews 4:12 tells us the power of the Word as a weapon, declaring, "For the word of God is quick, and powerful, and sharper than any twoedged sword, piercing even to the dividing asunder of soul and spirit, and of the joints and marrow, and is a discerner of the thoughts and intents of the heart" (KJV).

This is not a fight against a person; this is a war with a spirit. People go years living with tension in their relationships. We harbor ill feelings toward certain people because of what they have done to us. To get at the root, you have to make sure confrontation is aimed in the appropriate direction. I've seen people spend valuable time confronting people, unaware that something spiritual was occurring behind the scenes. Jesus' confrontation helps us all understand the importance of addressing the right audience.

You cannot confront spirits if you are timid. You must have a level of confidence that causes you to approach the moment with the authority you have been given through Jesus Christ. Jesus tells us the level of authority we walk in as believers:

And these signs shall follow them that believe; in my name shall they cast out devils; they shall speak with new tongues; they shall take up serpents; and if they

drink any deadly thing, it shall not hurt them; they
shall lay hands on the sick, and they shall recover.
—MARK 16:17–18, KJV

Spiritual warfare is not some simulated religious exercise. This battle is real, and you must be prepared. Earlier in this book I mentioned a story about seven sons of Sceva that speaks to the need to be ready for spiritual warfare. Let me elaborate. Here is the story again:

> Now God worked unusual miracles by the hands of Paul, so that even handkerchiefs or aprons were brought from his body to the sick, and the diseases left them and the evil spirits went out of them. Then some of the itinerant Jewish exorcists took it upon themselves to call the name of the Lord Jesus over those who had evil spirits, saying, "We exorcise you by the Jesus whom Paul preaches." Also there were seven sons of Sceva, a Jewish chief priest, who did so. And the evil spirit answered and said, "Jesus I know, and Paul I know; but who are you?" Then the man in whom the evil spirit was leaped on them, overpowered them, and prevailed against them, so that they fled out of that house naked and wounded.
> —ACTS 19:11–16

If you are not prepared for confrontation, it is best to wait until you are. When you are grounded in your faith through the Word of God, have a strong prayer life, and walk in spiritual confidence, you are ready. If there is timidity, superficial biblical knowledge, and an inconsistent prayer life, you are not ready. Unclean spirits have the ability to transfer, and if you are not guarded, the very thing you are trying to cast out of someone else's life can end up in your house. Your prayer life keeps you guarded. You cannot confront unclean spirits without being constantly connected to God in prayer for yourself. Your personal prayer life allows you to seek God's guidance as well as His help while seeking deliverance. When you pray, you have the ability to ask God for what you need. If you want to be set free, ask Him.

This is why you can't let everybody pray for you. You need people who are consecrated and prepared in the area of spiritual warfare to the degree that even demons know who they are. Jesus never had to announce Himself. The unclean spirit in the man in Mark 5 ran to Him and declared that He was the Son of God. People recognize your titles, but spirits recognize your authority. The worst thing you can ever do is have a long list of ecclesiastical and secular titles but no recognizable authority in the spirit realm. Your spiritual authority is developed through your convictions, character, and commitment. When you stand firmly on God's Word, you establish God's authority as your own. Your character aligns with your convictions and causes you to live above reproach. Your spiritual influence is directly tied to your character. I've said on numerous occasions that there can be no commitment where there is no character. People of high character demonstrate high levels of commitment. Your authority as a believer is related to having all these characteristics present in your life.

Jesus not only confronted this unclean spirit by speaking directly to it, but He also commanded it to come out. The command was more than an instruction; it was a declaration of ownership. Jesus was essentially saying that the man didn't belong to Satan; he belonged to God. When Satan attacks a life, his intentions are to set up permanent residence. He has every intention of remaining in the attack until his objectives are realized. You and I have to remind ourselves daily that we belong to God. Psalm 100:3 tells us to "know that the LORD, He is God; it is He who has made us, and not we ourselves; we are His people and the sheep of His pasture."

You are God's creation designed with an amazing purpose and destiny. This is what makes you such a target for the enemy. He not only is trying to torment and suppress your life, but he also wants to derail your destiny. The longer he controls your life, the more damage he can cause, thus preventing God's intentions from coming to fruition. Who knows what this man would have accomplished in life had this spirit not overtaken him.

We often think spiritual attacks and struggles are a consequence of something a person did. The enemy actually targets people who have an incredible future. Jesus told Peter in Luke 22:31–32: "Simon, Simon! Indeed, Satan has asked for you, that he may sift you as wheat. But I have prayed for you, that your faith should not fail; and when you have returned to Me, strengthen your brethren." Why did Jesus say this to Peter and not the other disciples? I know I've asked, "Why me?" You may have asked that question as well. Satan desired to sift Peter because he would be the one

Jesus would build His church upon. He would be the one who would proclaim the gospel on the day of Pentecost. He would be a significant leader in the first-century church.

Satan is very rarely attacking you because of what's happening in your life now. It's more likely that he is attacking you because of what's in your future. If you are experiencing spiritual attack, rather than be discouraged, you should use it as confirmation that he sees your future as a threat to his kingdom. If Satan doesn't attack you, it should make you nervous because it suggests he doesn't see anything of value worth derailing.

Although the man in the tombs had been under attack for some time, the purpose of the confrontation between Jesus and the legion was to normalize and stabilize his life. Jesus was serving the unclean spirits an eviction notice. Perhaps you are reading this and you are beyond weary of the demonic residence in your life. The struggles you are constantly having to fight are a result of the unclean spirits' comfort in your life. Today is the day you have to declare, "Come out!" But they won't come out until you come out of the tombs of your situation. When you come out of your tombs and meet the power of Jesus, you will be healed, set free, and delivered. You must make the first step toward your deliverance. You must ask yourself, "How bad do I want to be free of this?"

Jesus is not coming in the tombs with you. Jesus is not in the business of going inside dead places. Even when His dear friend Lazarus died, Jesus did not go inside the tomb and pull him out. Jesus stood outside the tomb and called Lazarus out. The Scriptures say, "And when [Jesus] thus had spoken, he cried with a loud voice, Lazarus, come forth. And he that was dead came forth, bound hand and foot with graveclothes: and his face was bound about with a napkin. Jesus saith unto them, Loose him, and let him go" (John 11:43–44, KJV).

Jesus will call you out of the tombs to deliver you and set you free of your dead situation. There is a moment in all our lives when the Holy Spirit will make us so uncomfortable in our mess that we start seeking deliverance. This is the work of the Holy Spirit to convict us so we see the need for change. And if you let Him be Lord of your life, He can keep you out of the tombs. But you must have a noncompromising approach and be willing to do what is necessary to experience the freedom you deserve in Christ.

EXERCISE YOUR AUTHORITY IN CHRIST

One of the things many believers fail to realize is the scope of authority we have. Jesus says in Luke 10:19, "I have given you authority to trample on snakes and scorpions and to overcome all the power of the enemy; nothing will harm you" (NIV). Jesus is telling us that all the powers of the enemy are subject to us and that we have authority to prevail in any circumstance. I heard a story years ago about authority that has helped me put this concept in perspective. A man called his pastor to inform him that he had a demon in his house. The pastor questioned the man concerning the activity of the demon. The man informed him that the spirit made his floor shake violently, threw items throughout the house, and made the windows go up and down. The pastor was convinced the man was dealing with a demon and made an appointment to go and cast the evil spirit out. Upon his arrival the evil spirit did exactly what the man described. The floor shook violently, and things were being thrown across the room. The pastor took out his anointing oil and said with a loud cry, "Come out!"

Suddenly the room went still. It appeared the evil spirit was finally gone. The man embraced his pastor and thanked him for finally casting out the evil spirit. The pastor was determined to teach the man a lesson on authority and did something rather bizarre. He cried out with a loud voice and said, "Devil, get back in here." The man was bewildered and frightened at the same time. When the demon returned, it was twice as violent as it was before. Items flew across the room and the floor shook violently, dislocating much of the furniture. The man asked his pastor why he would summon the evil spirit back in. The pastor's next statement explained it all. He cried once again with a loud voice and said, "Devil, before you came in, my member's bed was against that wall, his sofa was in that corner, and his silverware was in that drawer. Put it back."

When you think of the authority God wants you to have when you confront demonic spirits, it is not just authority to tell a spirit to leave; it is also the power to command it to put things back in place. Tell the unclean spirit to put back your ministry, your marriage, and your money. You have to remind the unclean spirit that has attacked you that your house, family, possessions, and everything else belong to God. Your tolerance has run its course, and this spirit must come out.

It is also important to note that Jesus called out the spirit for what it was. He called it an unclean spirit. To call it unclean is to give us permission to call the attack upon our lives exactly what it is. In her book *Clean House—Strong House* Kimberly Daniels, pastor of Spoken Word Ministries in Jacksonville, Florida, shares the importance of knowing the names of demons. She writes:

> In Mark 5:9, the word *name* is *onoma* in the Greek. According to the meaning of this word, Jesus asked the demon:
>
> - What are you called?
> - What is your authority?
> - What is your character?
>
> The word *onoma* means, "What are you called in the spirit? What is your character? By what authority do you operate?" This is how we destroy devils at Spoken Word. We identify them by name. Names are extremely important to demons. If a demon does not recognize the name of the person attempting to destroy it, that person has no authority over that demon.[1]

Demons know the name of Jesus. In Mark 1:23–24 the gospel writer gives an account of a demon that recognized Jesus and His authority, stating, "Now there was a man in their synagogue with an unclean spirit. And he cried out, saying, "Let us alone! What have we to do with You, Jesus of Nazareth? Did You come to destroy us? I know who You are—the Holy One of God!" Demons must know our names, and we must know the names of demons so we can take full authority over the operation of that spirit. The society we live in today often gives names to spirits that sugarcoat their real identity. This is an unclean spirit. When you say it, you own it. This is not just a bad day or a little drinking problem or a season when you had an unbridled sex life. Call it out for what it is. If you could look in the mirror and call out your issue, that would help you, because the more you acknowledge the spirit at the root of your dysfunction, the more you will despise its presence in your life.

It's not pretty and it is somewhat painful, but when you go through this process, it will pay huge dividends in your future. It's an addiction. It's promiscuity. It's cheating. It's lying. It's hypocrisy. To confront the spirit, you have to be honest about what it really is. You must deal with some attacks on your body in the same manner. Some sicknesses and diseases are a part of testing and trials of life, but you must learn to differentiate between a sickness that will call for only clinical assistance and a sickness that is a result of a demonic attack. This is why it's important to seek God in prayer so you can gain clarity concerning what you are facing.

As you continue to move closer to the root in your pursuit of restoration, remember that it is possible only through confrontation. The earth must be disturbed and dug up to get to the roots of the tree. The Lord told the prophet Jeremiah, "See, I have this day set you over the nations and over the kingdoms, to root out and to pull down, to destroy and to throw down, to build and to plant"

(Jer. 1:10). The work of the kingdom of God requires you to do intense root work. For God's kingdom to stand strong on the earth, the kingdoms of this world must be rooted out, pulled down, and destroyed. The root work must be done before a strong foundation can be built. The root work can be done only when you confront the problem by coming face to face with the underlying issues that would compromise what God wants to build in your life.

You can't put a building up before properly constructing the foundation. Confrontation is the essential step in moving you toward deliverance and ultimately the healing you desire. No confrontation will result in no revelation. Therefore you must come to a place where you declare, "This has to happen!" If you do not become clear on what is your core issue, you will not be ready to receive the revelation on how to become completely free of what is causing death in your life. What you fail to confront will fail to change in your life. The bottom line: no confrontation, no change. Longtime UCLA basketball coach John Wooden is often quoted as saying, "Failure is not fatal, but failure to change might be."[2]

You have to be willing to disturb the content and protest anything that threatens God's will for your life. As we approach the next chapter and perhaps the most difficult part of this process, remember your worth and God's promise to you in Jeremiah 29:11: "For I know the thoughts that I think toward you…thoughts of peace, and not of evil, to give you an expected end" (KJV). Take courage. The struggle is almost over.

ROOT WORK

1. Can you identify some things that make it difficult for you to confront the unclean spirits affecting your life?

2. What purpose in your life do you believe is being derailed because of the attacks of the enemy?

3. Do you believe you possess the power and authority to confront the demons that launch attacks against your life? Share some ways your convictions, character, and commitment play out in your everyday life.

4. What are the names of the unclean spirits that have come against you in the past? Make a three-column list. In the first column name the unclean spirit. In the second column list the actions of the unclean spirits. In the third column write down how you became free of that spirit.

5. Describe the moment when the Holy Spirit convicted you concerning the need for change in your life during a spiritual attack.

CHAPTER 8

Revelation:
Root Work

AFTER JESUS COMMANDED the spirit to leave the man in Mark 5, He immediately asked what I believe is the most important question in the entire exchange. He asked the unclean spirit, "What is your name?" As I mentioned earlier, this line of questioning was not to reveal anything new to Jesus; rather, it was to bring us into a greater revelation. I define *revelation* as the apprehension of truth at your own level of comprehension. Since we are journeying to the core of our issues, it is essential that we are able to completely apprehend truth as it is revealed. All the things you've experienced have prepared you to comprehend and apprehend the revelation that is about to come forth.

Let's admit it. Journeying to the core can be scary. There is so much uncertainty because you don't know what you might find. So many people have not been restored at the root because they fear the process. Think about this. If cancer is discovered in your body and you need to have surgery, your primary concern is that the physician will get it all. Nobody wants cancer removed from one area and neglected in another. This "get it all" approach is what root work is about. It's about the good, the bad, and the ugly. It's about opening up chapters of your life that have been sealed. It's about uncovering deep family secrets. It's about shedding light on the dark chapters of your past. It's about coming face to face with your fears.

Root work is excavation. It is digging until you arrive at the problem. You can't get well until you get to the problem. Understanding more details about the process of excavation will give you a clearer image of how having root work performed in your life will bring about transformation. Excavation is said to be "the most time-honored archaeological tool for understanding the processes of the human past."[1] *Excavation* is defined as "the controlled exploration of what lies below the surface, usually carried out systematically."[2]

Excavation is tedious work that will involve digging down through the surface, often progressing only one centimeter at a time. It can be very difficult, strenuous work. Excavation is not a walk in the park. It requires intense effort to get through layers of packed-down dirt. However, the ultimate purpose of excavation is to "reveal the types of human activities that took place at a site over time."[3] Those who are skilled in excavation, mainly archaeologists, can look back in time by examining the subject of their search. Although the material they gather may paint an incomplete picture, it will give researchers what they need to reconstruct the cultural history to determine what likely took place during a particular time in that particular place.

When you allow Jesus to do root work in your life, He essentially becomes a skilled archaeologist who will excavate the land of your soul to understand what issues in your past are causing the damaging effects in your present. It is the exploration of what is underneath the sleepless nights, incessant crying, screaming, depression, and uncontrolled behavior. Jesus gets to the core of your being by going beyond the surface and pulling back layer after layer.

We know that Jesus performed extensive root work on the man in Mark 5 because when He first encountered him, Jesus commanded the unclean spirits to leave. Jesus spoke to the one spirit that was speaking on behalf of the other demons tormenting the man. But Jesus knew there was more to the story. When He asked, "What is your name?" Jesus was pulling off another layer to reveal the other demonic spirits that were also at work in the man.

This was no drive-by deliverance. Just as archaeological excavation is a lengthy process, doing root work is an extensive process that is not for the faint of heart. You must learn to do as Paul instructed in 1 Corinthians 15:58 and "be steadfast, immovable, always abounding in the work of the Lord, knowing that your labor is not in vain in the Lord." It may take a while. You may get tired at times, but please know your faithfulness will produce great gain for you or the one who comes to you in need of deliverance.

Jesus' excavation continued, and as the unclean spirits continued to talk, it was clear that over the years multiple demons had taken up residence in the man. It was highly probable that some of the unclean spirits formed attachments to the man early in his life, quite possibly during his childhood. We are not provided with the man's age, but the number of demons residing in the man indicates he had been under demonic oppression for many years.

The man had a legion of demons within him. As a master human excavator Jesus knew that based on cultural history, a legion was a comparison to a band of Roman soldiers. A legion was no small group of men; in fact, it was a group of more than six thousand soldiers.[4] We are not informed of how long the process of assessing the number of demons in this man took, but we do know that Jesus took the time to do the work.

This unclean spirit had been the subject of numerous conversations within the community. Based on their many attempts to tie the man up, it is clear that the people of the Gadarenes discussed this man's condition. All they had to go on was what they saw. The spirit's violent manifestations and the man's dysfunctional reality created a certain perception and naming of his situation. Up to this point he had always been the man with the unclean spirit. It was assumed he was the victim of one spirit that was determined to destroy him. These assumptions were based on what the community saw.

It's tragic that we live in a world where society makes decisions based on what it sees rather than gaining a broader understanding of people's struggles. You may see a kid on the street hustling or a person failing in school and draw conclusions based on implicit bias rather than an awareness of the underlying causes at play in his or her life. There could be social, emotional, or spiritual issues at the root of the behavior you deem problematic.

There was a child in the third grade in my elementary school who would not sit down. The teachers were concerned because he would stand during class and disobey their request for him to be seated like the other students. The child was eventually suspended, and before he returned to class, the teacher decided to have a consultation with his parents. The teacher visited the child's home and, after being invited inside, received the biggest revelation of her life. The home had no chairs or sofas. There was nothing to sit on. The child had adjusted to doing everything standing up because that's all he knew.

In many cases we as a society misdiagnose the issues of people we consider problematic, and oftentimes they are dealing with unclean spirits that developed over time, due in part to the systemic problems of their environment. Those who are crying out from the tombs of their zone of the city may be in a fierce battle with generational demons that keep them bound to a variety of generational cycles such as substance abuse, sexual promiscuity, or a life of crime.

It is important to know that what you see with your natural eye does not tell the full story. Jesus' question is the essence of what I call root work—the willingness to go beyond the surface and get to the actual root of the matter. You will never get to the root if you are making conclusions based only on what you see.

Asking the demon its name imposed authority upon it and forced it to reveal its true nature. For years it had been assumed that this man had a single spirit, which is exactly what the demons wanted people to believe. Had Jesus not probed into what was truly tormenting this man, the deliverance could have been incomplete. You can never be content with a partial exit. The deliverance needs to be complete. But you will never fully understand a struggle, whether your own or someone else's, until you get an accurate picture of what is at the root.

ROOT WORK IS HARD WORK

Root work is difficult because it pushes past perceptions and operates only in the realm of truth. For the unclean spirit the masquerade is over. It must now come clean. It must now reveal who it really is. The Scripture tells us that God reveals hidden truths "through His Spirit. For the Spirit searches all things, yes, the deep things of God" (1 Cor. 2:10). If you want to be restored at the root, you are going to have to work through the emotions provoked by what emerges in the process. Root work will bring up painful memories, and you must be willing to press through those because it is part of the process of getting to a place of restoration. You are going to have to revisit things that occurred in your life years ago as well as be honest about how those events have affected your life. Root work gets to the core, and Jesus' question gives us all hope that restoration is possible.

Jesus asked, "What is your name?" And the demon replied, "My name is Legion; for we are many" (Mark 5:9). As I mentioned previously, this is a military term referring to a brigade. It also denotes that the demons were under orders. Military operations require strategic planning and tactical support, and demonic spirits often operate the same way. When Satan sends a legion in your life, those demons come with a strategic assignment and a barrage of calculated assaults. This man was not dealing with one isolated demon.

A platoon of many different demons had been hiding within him, with each wreaking a different kind of havoc in his life.

Root work is when you are willing to discover the layers of things that have created the dysfunction in your life. The struggles you've been facing were not caused by some isolated event. They are the result of the cumulative unresolved issues. When the unclean spirit revealed itself as many, it opened up a revelation concerning our own struggles. It is easy to label a thing based on what we see and completely miss the totality of what is causing the struggle. So many problems have been misdiagnosed and mislabeled, whether by others or by ourselves, because people were not willing to do root work. When you go beyond the surface and go after the legion, you will discover that a multitude of things have contributed to your current situation. Each of those things can lie deep at the root of your life, preventing you from experiencing deliverance.

When Jesus first encountered the man with the demons, only one spirit spoke; the others seemed to be hiding or lying dormant within the man. When something has been dormant for a long time, it may take a while to identify it. This appears to be the case with the unclean spirits operating in the man because when Jesus arrived in Gadara, only one actively engaged with Him, yet we learn that many were present. Do not be fooled when only one demon is acting out. Several others can be present; they simply may be lying dormant. When Jesus is engaged in root work, everything will come to the forefront. Even the things you forgot were an issue will rise up because it will be time for them to be expelled. This is why you must get out of the driver's seat and let Him lead you in the process. This will prevent you from avoiding the areas that are uncomfortable and moving at the right pace through those things that are necessary to confront.

When Jesus arrived on the scene, we were introduced to the legion of demons that had been controlling not only the man but also his entire territory. All six thousand-plus spirits began to speak at once, asking to be sent into the swine because they did not want to be expelled from the region. Whether they were controlling the region by terrorizing the people through this man or whether the spirits went in and out of this man, visiting other people in between, we know they were terrorizing this particular area.

Because no one in the region had been able to cast them out, the demons in this region had a strong power base. No one had ever commanded them to go; therefore they had become the ruling forces in this region. No one was able to contain or restrain the demons at work. Until you receive revelation on the unclean spirits that are at work in your life, you will not be in control; instead the demonic spirits will remain in the lead. You need revelation of what is actively going on in and around you so you can be free of the unclean spirits that want to continue ruling your life.

DON'T BE FOOLED BY WHAT LIES DORMANT

The interesting thing we must note about the demons that were what I call dormant is that they seemed to be at rest until they realized they were going to have to leave the man's body. These demons, especially this legion that functioned like soldiers, would be at rest only when their work had been completed. However, they remained in this man's body and were active only on an as-needed basis. Remember, 1 Peter 5:8 tells us that our adversary, the devil, walks about as "a roaring lion, seeking whom he may devour." Until the person is devoured or taken over completely, the devil will not cease to be active. Yet when the demonic spirit becomes fully confident in its complete takeover of that portion of the person's life, it will take a rest and allow the accompanying demons to take center stage.

The demons at rest had already taken over the man's ability to control himself. They had driven him into isolation and depravation. The demons we see at work when Jesus approached the area were now focused on total annihilation. The unclean spirits actively at work at this point in the man's life were causing him to cry out and cut himself. They were in complete control of the man. He had no control over basic functions such as thinking, speaking, or walking. Everything the man did when Jesus was present was directed by the unclean spirits within him.

You must realize that demons will not stop until they utterly destroy you. Therefore, if you are going to be set free from what is actively attacking your life right now, you must also become free of the things that have hurt you in the past. You are not free until every spirit that caused you pain is rooted out. What is often called residue, the leftover effects of unclean spirits in a person's life, has more than likely been a dormant demon. Residue is a small part of something that remains present after the main part of that particular thing has been removed. It cannot be considered residue if the spirit can fully manifest when the area in which it is resting is awakened. In essence, if you can be brought completely back into a behavior as if it had never been removed, that means it was never removed; it was simply dormant in your life.

You may have thought you were free from a person, place, or thing. But if, when presented with the opportunity, you were back in full engagement with that person or thing, or you found yourself blacked out, having allowed a substance to have full control over you, then you were not truly free. All it took was one look, one drink, one hit, and you were back where you were before you disconnected from that person or before you went to rehab the last time. Unless the spirit is rooted out, you cannot trust that it has gone just because you don't hear, feel, or see it. Like good soldiers the legion of demons will band together to accomplish their mission, and that agenda is usually to stay together and to remain in their place of residence.

Legion is the manifestation of the deeper issues in a person's life. For example, people may think their issue is with promiscuity. But dealing only with promiscuity leaves untouched the deeper issues that gave rise to that behavior. Perhaps it was the abuse they experienced when they were young. Or maybe it was low self-esteem coupled with their insecurities. If you cast out promiscuity, the demon will redirect to low self-esteem or something else. This is the root work. It answers the question, Why am I the way I am?

It delves deeper into your life and creates an opportunity for you to analyze the impact trauma may have had on you.

Can you imagine the number of people society has put into particular categories based on a shallow interpretation of their struggle? On the surface we see a person battling with anger. Behind the anger could be rejection, a violent home life, or loss. Root work is necessary because it not only helps us get to the source of our struggles; it also helps us perceive ourselves correctly. I was almost placed in special education classes when I was in elementary school. This classification would have impacted my life for many years. I admit I had a disciplinary problem. I had so much energy it caused me to act out in class. My teacher felt like my behavior warranted my taking a test to see if I needed to be in special education classes. I took the test, and it revealed that I was gifted. Behind my energy were boredom and self-esteem issues that caused me to act out for attention and validation. I'm able to admit that now because I did the root work years ago. The revelation is truly at the root. If our churches and society are going to do better, we must move beyond our initial reactions to people and be willing to explore what is happening at the root.

GOD WORKS THROUGH
PRAYER... AND THERAPISTS

One of the things we must come to grips with is how the historical models used to address life-controlling issues have failed us. I believe more than anyone that there is power in prayer. I believe in the power we have as believers to take authority over unclean spirits. Nevertheless, I also believe that when you are dealing with a legion, you must embrace the clinical resources that can help make sense of what has occurred in your life. The church has not always embraced clinical therapy, and as a consequence we've contributed to the erroneous perceptions regarding it. People think they are crazy if they go to therapy. I believe you are crazy if you don't go.

Another pervasive misperception concerning therapy is that if you go to counseling, your faith in God isn't strong and you don't believe He can get you through your crisis. This is where we must be mindful of the need for responsible teaching and preaching and help people understand the benefits of these resources. Counselors and therapists are not enemies to our faith; rather, they are companions in our faith walk to freedom, assisting us through those difficult seasons of our lives. Just as medical doctors have a calling on their lives to assist us with our physical health needs, psychiatrists and therapists are called to assist us with our mental health needs. God desires for you to live in complete wholeness. He doesn't want you to be spiritually strong yet mentally and emotionally broken. We hear the heart of God concerning His desire for us to be whole in 3 John 2, which says, "Beloved, I wish above all things that thou mayest prosper and be in health, even as thy soul prospereth" (KJV).

I've seen people who refused to receive help from a therapist and ended up at the church altar nearly every Sunday for the same problem. After leaders prayed over them, they continued their struggle because it was easier to have someone lay hands on them than to have someone guide them in probing the underlying issues in their heart. Often in our church services people are looking for a magical, abracadabra approach rather than going through the process of root work. Just as God will use medical doctors to help you diagnose a physical problem, He also uses Christian clinical counselors to help you identify the root of the dysfunction in your life and reconcile the events from your past.

Many people already recognize the connection between their mental and emotional well-being and their spiritual well-being, which may help explain why there has been an increase in the number of Christian counselors in recent years. Studies have shown that people prefer counselors who share their faith and will not challenge their beliefs. People who practice a particular faith often complain that counselors see their faith as a problem or a symptom of something they are dealing with, and as a consequence they prefer to see counselors who share their religious beliefs. According to a nationwide survey by the American Association of Pastoral Counselors, "83 percent of Americans believe their spiritual faith and religious beliefs are closely tied to their state of mental and emotional health." This is likely why "three-fourths say it's important for them to see a professional counselor who integrates their values and beliefs into the counseling process."[5]

There are many therapists who are Christians and have solid credentials to treat mental and emotional needs. There is a growing need for churches to raise awareness of mental health needs and serve as advocates for those who need professional help. Mental Health Awareness Month is recognized each May, and it is a great opportunity for church communities to speak out about the effects of mental illness. If you are a pastor, your congregation has likely been longing for you speak out about this. LifeWay research found that a majority of churchgoing families (65 percent) want their churches to talk openly about mental illness, but nearly half of pastors surveyed (49 percent) rarely or never address the subject. Only 27 percent of churches had a plan to help families affected by mental health issues. Consider that in light of the fact that nearly a third of churchgoers (32 percent) know someone, either a close acquaintance or a relative, who has died as a result of suicide, and only 35 percent say mental illness can be overcome solely through prayer and Bible study.[6]

These statistics coupled with the rise in the suicide rate in our communities and churches should serve as an indication that the church needs to speak more openly about mental health. It is time for the church to stop viewing therapy and counseling as taboo. Healing is found in God, and He has called and raised up many professionals to help us find that healing through clinical means. Without an expert to help you navigate this tough terrain, it can be difficult to discover the interrelatedness of these events. When you have experienced trauma, you can't sweep it under the rug. You have to walk through that circumstance and understand how Satan can use it—and likely *is* using it—to advance his agenda.

A WORD TO LEADERS

Before I go on, I want to say a word concerning high-level leaders such as pastors, CEOs, celebrities, and the like. I have been a pastor for more than twenty-five years, and I am very aware of the challenges and mindsets associated with leadership. The demands and expectations of their positions can cause leaders to lose sight of themselves and make them targets of demonic exploitation. The trauma they may have experienced tends to be masked by their exceptional abilities to perform their duties. But it is crucial that these sorts of leaders remain aware of the unique ways Satan executes attacks upon their lives. By examining the effect leadership had on Moses as seen in Exodus chapter 18, we can identify the spiritual minefields leaders must be careful to avoid.

Moses was isolated from his family.

Verses 2–4 say, "Then Jethro, Moses' father-in-law, took Zipporah, Moses' wife, after he had sent her back, with her two sons, of whom the name of one was Gershom (for he said, 'I have been a stranger in a foreign land') and the name of the other was Eliezer (for he said, 'The God of my father was my help, and delivered me from the sword of Pharaoh')."

The word *sent* used in verse 2 implies that Moses was separated from his family. Often the demands of leadership pull us away from our families, but this can have devastating results. Because Moses was away from his family, he likely was not able to pour into his sons as a father should. We must realize that the enemy is after not just us;

he is also after the next generation. Neglecting our families exposes them to spiritual attack.

I believe being away from his family also put Moses' marriage on the rocks. Verse 2 says Moses sent his wife back, suggesting he was unable to incorporate her into his ministry. Zipporah was a Midianite whom he met when he was running from Pharaoh. Moses' wife represents escape. Family should be our escape. We need our families so we can escape the constant pull of ministry. However, the enemy wants us to escape our families and be consumed with our assignments. We must be intentional about preserving our most important relationships.

Moses was consumed by his ministry identity.

We read in verses 8 and 13: "And Moses told his father-in-law all that the LORD had done to Pharaoh and to the Egyptians for Israel's sake, all the hardship that had come upon them on the way, and how the LORD had delivered them.... And so it was, on the next day, that Moses sat to judge the people; and the people stood before Moses from morning until evening." Many leaders have a deep need to be needed, but the attention they receive feeds something within them that causes them to lose focus. Once we lose focus, Satan can manipulate us by exploiting our vulnerabilities and causing us to act out in ways that are inconsistent with who we are truly called to be. Moses was like many leaders who struggle to find personal time apart from the demands of their assignments. Life in the proverbial fishbowl can have serious implications upon our time spent with God and our families. This, again, is why we must be intentional about recharging through prayer and Bible study, creating time for our families.

Moses had a distorted perception of ministry.

Again, verse 13 says, "And so it was, on the next day, that Moses sat to judge the people; and the people stood before Moses from morning until evening." Moses was taking on too much under the assumption that he could fix everyone's problems. We are not called to be God, only to serve Him and watch Him work in the lives of His people. Trying to take God's glory for himself led to Lucifer's fall, and doing the same will open a wide door for spiritual attack.

Moses had an inflated sense of importance.

We read in verses 14–15, "So when Moses' father-in-law saw all that he did for the people, he said, 'What is this thing that you are doing for the people? Why do you alone sit, and all the people stand before you from morning until evening?' And Moses said to his father-in-law, 'Because the people come to me to inquire of God.'" Leaders are often pushed into roles that create a false sense of indispensability. We should approach our assignments with humility because God could have chosen anybody, but He chose us. We cannot think we are irreplaceable or invincible. This arrogance appeals to Satan and his agenda in our lives.

Moses misplaced his priorities.

Verse 16 says, "When they have a difficulty, they come to me, and I judge between one and another; and I make known the statutes of God and His laws." The use of the pronoun *I* indicates that Moses, like so many leaders, forgot that it's God who does the work, not us. We are mere vessels for His glory. If we forget that, our pride will bring our downfall (Prov. 16:18).

Moses was overloaded and burned out.

Exodus 18:17 goes on to say, "So Moses' father-in-law said to him, 'The thing that you do is not good.'" Moses was carrying too much. Often we don't delegate and as a result burn ourselves out. When we are physically or emotionally spent, we become easy prey for spiritual attack.

Moses stressed/distressed himself and the people he served.

Verse 18 says, "Thou wilt surely wear away, both thou, and this people that is with thee: for this thing is too heavy for thee; thou art not able to perform it thyself alone" (KJV). When a leader is stressed, he or she creates a stressful environment. This becomes a portal the enemy can use to attack our lives.

Moses micromanaged.

Moses' training in Egypt taught him how to be a controlling leader. This is an unhealthy model of leadership. When we are exposed to dysfunctional models, we often attempt to replicate those in our current contexts, but we do so at a great risk. Satan is quick to latch on to any kind of dysfunction. Whether it is control, narcissism, or any other dysfunctional trait we pick up along the way, it makes us vulnerable to spiritual attack.

Moses used an oppressive ministry model.

Jethro, Moses' father-in-law, told him,

> Listen now to my voice; I will give you counsel, and
> God will be with you: Stand before God for the
> people, so that you may bring the difficulties to God.
> And you shall teach them the statutes and the laws,
> and show them the way in which they must walk and
> the work they must do. Moreover you shall select
> from all the people able men, such as fear God, men
> of truth, hating covetousness; and place such over
> them to be rulers of thousands, rulers of hundreds,
> rulers of fifties, and rulers of tens. And let them judge
> the people at all times. Then it will be that every great
> matter they shall bring to you, but every small matter
> they themselves shall judge. So it will be easier for
> you, for they will bear the burden with you.
>
> —EXODUS 18:19–22

Moses did as his father-in-law instructed and ended
up operating in a hierarchical ministry model rather
than a relational one. In hierarchical models relationships are positioned over and under; someone has to be
over us. However, relational models assume someone is
working beside us. When we are not spiritually grounded,
authority can get the best of us, causing pride to emerge.
Again, pride always puts us at risk for spiritual attack.

When we examine Moses' leadership and the demands
placed upon him, we can clearly see why many leaders
get burned out or lose passion. They have to constantly

guard against the enemy's attempt to sabotage their purpose. Many leaders are experiencing family breakdown, ministry breakdown, physical breakdown, nervous breakdown, moral breakdown, and spiritual breakdown. With these constant challenges and demands it is clear that even leaders need to talk it out with someone who can assist.

As a pastor I advocate for clinical counseling. After losing my first wife to cancer, I contemplated counseling for months, but I kept convincing myself that I could deal with the grief and pull through. When I finally submitted to the process of counseling, I was able to see deeper issues I was harboring that could have had potentially devastating effects on my future. I discovered issues of guilt because I thought I could have been a better husband. I discovered issues of spiritual insecurity because I felt my prayers were impotent, thus contributing to my wife's passing. Yet as painful as these and many other revelations were, uncovering them was essential to my healing process.

It was difficult to unravel all the things that had occurred and work through my emotions, but it was necessary. Going to counseling did not jeopardize my faith; it enhanced it. It gave me a clear picture of what I was dealing with and how I could overcome it. I didn't go to counseling as a pastor; I went as a person. Regardless of your title or job position, don't lose sight of your humanity. You are a real person dealing with real issues. You don't have to be a spiritual superhero. It's OK to acknowledge when something is too much for you to figure out.

I was accustomed to fixing things. When people came to me, I felt I could fix any problem, yet I eventually realized

I couldn't fix myself. Counseling is a gift from God. It's one of the most powerful tools of root work. If you are reading this and you know you need to talk to somebody, don't wait another day. Find someone you can trust. Do your research. You will discover that there is a specialist in the area of your struggle. Let the Word of God do what it's designed to do, and allow a counselor to do his or her part. You will be amazed at the results.

ROOT WORK

1. List three areas of vulnerability in your life the enemy has used to launch an attack against you.

2. Have past issues caused you to be unfairly misdiagnosed or labeled? If so, what behaviors might have contributed to those labels?

3. Have you been affected by the partial exit of an unclean spirit? Can you identify the damage the enemy caused upon its departure?

4. After reading this chapter, explain how you see the relationship between clinical counseling and spiritual warfare.

5. Identify specific ways you are currently engaged in root work.

CHAPTER 9

Enumeration:
What Is It Worth to You?

NOW THAT YOU have a revelation of the scope of the attack upon your life, it's important that we address the issue of enumeration. How much is being completely free worth to you? After Jesus exposed the legion at work in the man's life, the unclean spirits made a request that reveals the cost associated with root work.

> He begged Him earnestly that He would not send them out of the country. Now a large herd of swine was feeding there near the mountains. So all the demons begged Him, saying, "Send us to the swine, that we may enter them." And at once Jesus gave them permission. Then the unclean spirits went out and entered the swine (there were about two thousand); and the herd ran violently down the steep place into the sea, and drowned in the sea.
>
> —MARK 5:10–13

The unclean spirits going into the swine represent a loss of revenue for the swineherd. We will look closer at that in a moment, but we must first understand this unusual request from the unclean spirits. The legion recognized it had to depart, but it asked Jesus to allow it to stay in that area.

I've often said that demons are assigned to places or regions. Although the spirits knew they had to vacate this man, they wanted to stay in the town of Gadara. Perhaps a culture in the region was conducive to harboring unclean spirits. When we examine the community's inability to cast the unclean spirits out and their willingness to let them operate on the outskirts of society, one can see why the demons would want to remain. Gadara must have felt like a refuge. Because Legion was a military demon, we must understand that it was most concerned about regional occupation. The man was merely a casualty of war.

In the negotiation phase spirits are more apt to give up the person than the land. To give up the land is to acknowledge complete defeat. Demons are battling for dominion. Remember God said in Genesis 1:26, "Let Us make man in Our image, according to Our likeness; let them have dominion over the fish of the sea, over the birds of the air, and over the cattle, over all the earth and over every creeping thing that creeps on the earth." God has given you dominion in the earth, or the authority to occupy and control territory.

When you examine the request of the unclean spirits, it becomes apparent that regions do not have fixed boundaries and that authority is always subject to jurisdiction. If the demons could continue to occupy that region, the area would remain under their authority. In Ephesians 6:12, when Paul referred to principalities, he was referring to spirits that rule over territories. This means demons don't just want to torment you; they want to take over the area where you reside. The unclean spirits want to take over your communities; your job; your local schools; and your house, spouse, and kids with a mouse.

This is a serious issue, especially concerning how much demonic activity technology enables children to access. With a click of a computer mouse your child can be transported into an entire cyber world. Much of what it presents is beneficial information, but many dark forces lurk within cyberspace. Adults disguising themselves as teenagers or other children may be trying to lure our kids into a world of sexual exploitation and other dark acts that could lead to their demise. If we do not place controls on what our children can access through their phones, tablets, and laptops, they will become victims of the all-out demonic attack that has been launched against this generation.

Matthew 26:41 instructs us to "watch and pray, that ye enter not into temptation: the spirit indeed is willing, but the flesh is weak" (KJV). We must pray over our families, but we must also be on the watch for the attacks that would seek to lure our family members into sin and trap them in bondage. The apostle Paul wrote in 1 Corinthians 10:13, "No temptation has overtaken you except such as is common to man; but God is faithful, who will not allow you to be tempted beyond what you are able, but with the temptation will also make the way of escape, that you may be able to bear it."

The way to escape temptation as a Christian is much like the evacuation plan organizations follow in an emergency situation such as a fire:

1. **Find the nearest exit.** Get out of the situation and get to a place of safety as quickly as possible. The apostle Paul told Timothy to "flee also youthful lusts" (2 Tim. 2:22). Even if you have to run, get away from the temptation as fast as you can.

2. **Protect yourself from the effects of what is going on around you.** Stay covered in prayer.

3. **Call for help if you can't get out by yourself.** If the situation is too powerful for you to handle on your own, call for assistance. Find others who will cover you in prayer and help you find a way of escape.

4. **Get to a safe place as soon as possible.** Once you remove yourself from the temptation, get to a place of safety and stay there. Don't go back to the tempting situation.

5. **Once you have left the troublesome situation, do an assessment of your well-being.** Depending on the extent of the exposure to the unclean spirits, you may need treatment. This may come in the form of spiritual renewal or counseling.

In many cases of emergency there is an evacuation leader. The role of the evacuation leader is to make sure everyone follows the procedures in place for times of emergency. You may have a person in your life who serves as an evacuation leader to help guide you through emergency situations. It may be your pastor, your prayer partner, your spouse, or a family member who can help walk you through this process. Or you may be that person for others.

During times of temptation or spiritual attack, it is important to remember to do the following:

- **Keep calm.** Isaiah 41:10 says, "Fear not, for I am with you; be not dismayed, for I am your God. I will strengthen you, yes, I will help you, I will uphold you with My righteous right hand." Panic will cause you to respond emotionally and put yourself in even more danger.

- **Keep walking.** The psalmist David encouraged us to keep walking past the situations that desire to lead us into temptation or destruction by letting us know that God is with us, even if we are in dangerous territory. He wrote in Psalm 23:4, "Yea, though I walk through the valley of the shadow of death, I will fear no evil; for You are with me; Your rod and Your staff, they comfort me."

- **Keep your focus.** During times of crisis, it is crucial that you remain focused so the distractions do not trap you into giving in to the temptation that will lead you to indulge in sin. Instead, when you are focused on where God wants you to go, you will be

led to a path of destiny and not destruction. Proverbs 4:25 shows us how to remain
focused through its instruction to "let your
eyes look straight ahead, and your eyelids
look right before you."

The struggle that occurs in so many regions, territories, cities, and communities is because many have lost sight of this tactical demonic assault. If we are to get to the root, we must be willing to make significant investments in the areas where demons have taken up residence. When we look at communities that have generational suffering, often there are no community centers. The schools within impoverished neighborhoods are frequently limited in the amount of financial resources they receive from their state and local governments. Recent studies have shown that "in more than half of the states in the U.S., the poorest school districts do not receive funding to address their students' increased needs.... School districts with the highest rates of poverty receive about $1,000 less per student in state and local funding than those with the lowest rates of poverty."[1] Often there also are food deserts within these impoverished communities, and the residents cannot buy quality, fresh, healthy food. In most cities demons have occupied entire streets with the intent to systematically destroy those communities.

In communities hard hit by demonic oppression, you typically will find restaurants with the kinds of food choices that contribute to many preventable diseases. There is usually a liquor store to get the people drunk enough and a drug house to get them high enough to anesthetize themselves from the dysfunction that surrounds them. There is a payday loan company to get them in a perpetual state of indebtedness and a funeral home to bury them when the stress of their circumstances puts them in an early grave. In Genesis, when God commanded humankind to have dominion over the earth, He didn't give them dominion over one another. People were never intended to have dominion over one another. Humans were never meant to be dominated; even God gives us free will so we can choose to follow Him. But unclean spirits desire to remain in certain territories so they control the destiny of the people who live within those areas.

In urban communities and areas we categorize as ghettos, demons are brazen and audacious. They dwell in the open and can be seen affecting social systems such as the criminal justice system and the economic system in the form of predatory lending businesses. Although it would be less costly in the long run if businesses invested in creating jobs in low-income areas, the unclean spirits operating through the economic system keep businesses in these areas in pursuit of immediate financial gain, even if their goods or services weaken the community and perpetuate generational poverty.

In her book *The Rules of Engagement: The Art of Strategic Prayer and Spiritual Warfare* Dr. Cindy Trimm points out that the kingdom of darkness has a sophisticated economy. She writes:

As with any other earthly kingdom, it trades and transacts business. Satan has built an entire evil empire by utilizing the most precious of all commodities—intellectual properties and the very souls of men. When it comes to humanity, many people have replaced their love of God with the love of money. First Timothy 6:10 declares, "For the love of money is the root of all evil: which while some coveted after, they have erred from the faith, and pierced themselves through with many sorrows." Throughout history we can trace many sinful, unholy, and ungodly activities and atrocities to this inordinate affection and idolatrous stronghold in the minds of men. Like the black widow spider that lures her prey to its demise in her web, this satanic economic system will lure any and every soul it can into a web designed for death and destruction.[2]

The oppressive economic system at work in low-income communities would rather make more money now on the backs of poor people than help to create a business model that would foster economic growth and positively influence those who live within that area. To change this corrupt system, businesses with a focus on bringing positive change to the community must be created to rid poor neighborhoods in particular of the darkness hidden within businesses that withdraw more from the community than they contribute. Nonprofit organizations such as economic development corporations should be created to help stimulate growth and attract new business to at-risk and impoverished communities. Putting a plan in place to stimulate healthy growth within a community will lead to the increase of schools, day care centers, grocery stores, and community centers for youth and families. Failure to create these types of businesses where economic development and growth are designed to bring positive change to the community will result in a much costlier remedy years down the road as communities work to combat the damaging effects of a negative economic system.

While the work of unclean spirits is often apparent in urban communities, demons are at work in suburban areas as well. Within many of these communities are gated neighborhoods where greedy and haughty demons reside. The terrible danger of these territorial demons is that they deceive people into having a false sense of security. The residents think they can control who or what gets in and out of their neighborhoods, but Legion has already encroached on their gates. The residents boast in their ability to guard themselves against flesh and blood, but they are defenseless against principalities, powers, and rulers of darkness.

The prophet Amos gave a stern warning against this spirit of complacency, saying:

> Woe to you who are at ease in Zion, and trust in Mount Samaria, notable persons in the chief nation, to whom the house of Israel comes! Go over to Calneh and see; and from there go to Hamath the great; then go down to Gath of the Philistines. Are you better than these kingdoms? Or is their territory greater than your territory? Woe to you who put

far off the day of doom, who cause the seat of violence to come near; who lie on beds of ivory, stretch
out on your couches, eat lambs from the flock and
calves from the midst of the stall; who sing idly to
the sound of stringed instruments, and invent for
yourselves musical instruments like David; who
drink wine from bowls, and anoint yourselves with
the best ointments, but are not grieved for the afflic-
tion of Joseph. Therefore they shall now go captive
as the first of the captives, and those who recline at
banquets shall be removed.

—Amos 6:1–7

Complacency is both dangerous and sinful. This is why
God detests the lukewarm. God sent the following message to the church of the Laodiceans in Revelation 3:15–16:
"I know your works, that you are neither cold nor hot. I
could wish you were cold or hot. So then, because you are
lukewarm, and neither cold nor hot, I will vomit you out
of My mouth." Those who are neither hot nor cold will be
vomited out of the mouth of God.

This is not the time in our society to be neutral on spiritual matters. You have to learn how to take a firm stand
for what you believe because, as the old adage says, "If you
don't stand for something, you will fall for anything."

Getting to the source of the issues that are plaguing
the world in which we live today is going to cost something. The question that must be asked is, Do you want to
pay now or later? You might say you can't give up doing a
particular thing that you know is causing unclean spirits

to run rampant in your life, but the reality is you cannot afford not to put an end to what is going on. You might say you can't give up a relationship that you know is unhealthy or a substance that is detrimental to your health. But you must understand that if you continue allowing unclean spirits to prevail, what you will lose now cannot be compared to what you will lose later. You can lose your home, your family, your job, your wealth, your social status, and even your life if you do not dismiss the demons in your life.

These foul and treacherous spirits were never meant to live among us, and they certainly are not supposed to live within you. When unclean spirits suppress Christians, they suppress the Spirit of God within those individuals, which causes them to live in a constant state of torment. The constant state of torment is a result of a foreign spirit being housed in a place that should be welcoming only to the Holy Spirit. Your body was created to house the Spirit of the living God, and allowing anything other than the Spirit of God to control you causes a major disruption in the earth.

> For the earnest expectation of the creation eagerly waits for the revealing of the sons of God. For the creation was subjected to futility, not willingly, but because of Him who subjected it in hope; because the creation itself also will be delivered from the bondage of corruption into the glorious liberty of the children of God. For we know that the whole creation groans and labors with birth pangs together until now. Not only that, but we also who have the

> firstfruits of the Spirit, even we ourselves groan
> within ourselves, eagerly waiting for the adoption,
> the redemption of our body.
>
> —Romans 8:19–23

Jesus refused to allow the unclean spirits to remain in the man, which led to their expulsion from his body and subsequently from the area where he resided. Jesus' command for the demons to come out of the man not only brought deliverance to him, but it also caused future generations to be free of the unclean spirits that sought to take up residence in the region.

WHAT IS FREEDOM WORTH TO YOU?

When Jesus cast the legion out of the man, He commanded it to enter some swine feeding in a field. The swine represent another aspect of the process. The unclean spirits asked to enter the swine because spirits need a vessel to occupy. This was an interesting request because the unclean spirits asked to inhabit something the Jewish people historically would have viewed as unclean. The irony is that although swine were viewed as unclean, the community allowed them to graze there. They protected them. This is because the people were protecting their investment. The people of this city had learned to accommodate something that was unclean, and they were apprehensive that Jesus had come to disrupt the entire system they had developed.

It is believed that because the people were allowing swineherds to dwell in the city, the people in this text were Gentiles. This gives us an even more expansive view of Jesus' ministry. If indeed this man was a Gentile, we see the work of Jesus going beyond the Jewish people to include delivering people who at the time were not connected to Jesus, the promised Jewish Messiah. Later in the text this very same man will be found proclaiming the works of Christ—but this occurred only because Jesus didn't bypass the man but took the time to heal and deliver him.

There are many views about why Jesus honored the demons' request and allowed them to go into the herd of swine. I believe Jesus allowed the spirits to enter the swine to allow the people in the city to witness the extreme and violent nature of the unclean spirits. Some people will let themselves think the situation isn't all that bad, that they aren't really in bondage. Or they will convince themselves that you were exaggerating about your life among the tombs. I've had people question the legitimacy and severity of my experiences. Perhaps you have too. Though some people do embellish their pain because they like attention, what you experienced was real.

The demons that had been harassing this man violently drove the pigs down the hill to their deaths. Imagine something that intense being in someone's life for who knows how long. What was cast out of one man caused the deaths of two thousand pigs. Living within this man was enough demonic violence to destroy an entire herd of swine. Demonic spirits have no other agenda than to steal from you, kill your hopes and dreams, and destroy your life. Unclean spirits have no good intentions toward you.

It appears the unclean spirits deduced that if they went into the swine, they would at least be protected. Jesus allowed this because He had no intentions of perpetuating what the community had done for years. Two thousand pigs ran violently down the hill and drowned in the sea. If you were the swineherd, the loss would seem even greater. Going down that hill into the water were literally thousands of hams, pork chops, spare ribs, and pigs' feet. In short, an economic impact is felt when unclean spirits are cast out. If you are serious about doing the real work necessary to be restored at the root, you have to decide what true, lasting freedom is worth to you.

There are communal investments in a church, but there is also a personal investment. We live in a world in which we spend billions of dollars on maintaining or improving our appearance yet we make minimal investment in addressing the internal. This is why we have so many pretty, ugly people. We look amazing on the outside, but we are a wreck on the inside. Our society spends billions on arenas to entertain us, yet most local government budgets barely provide enough funding to educate our children.

I believe your budget makes a theological statement. You will invest in what is important to you. The Bible says in Matthew 6:21, "For where your treasure is, there your heart will be also." The economic loss represented in the deaths of two thousand swine speaks to the investment Jesus was willing to make into one man's life. Jesus cares so much about you that He went to Calvary to prove His love to you. There is never a question of how much God is willing to invest; He sacrificed His Son so you could spend eternity with Him. The question is, What are you willing to invest in your deliverance? If you are ready to make the great investment toward walking in freedom, here are a few steps to be followed:

- **Invest the time.** You have to be willing to devote time to your deliverance. Your initial thought might be that you do not have the time to deal with the unclean spirits in your life, but the truth is you cannot afford to allow the unclean spirits to continue to run rampant in your life. Doing so will lead only to more extensive long-term damaging effects.

- **Invest the resources.** Your physical resources of energy and your financial resources may be required to help support your deliverance process. In a situation where your family member or friend may need help walking through the process of deliverance, it may cause you to devote physical resources in the form of being present when the person is experiencing withdrawals or going through rehab. In cases where it is you or a loved one, you may have to contribute financial resources toward treatment that will lead to deliverance. Be willing to invest the resources it takes to experience freedom.

- **Invest in the relationships.** You cannot do this alone. You will need people to help

support you and keep you accountable
during the deliverance process. Galatians
6:1–2 shares this with us regarding the need
for relationship support when a person is
caught up in sin: "Brothers and sisters, if
someone is caught in a sin, you who live by
the Spirit should restore that person gently.
But watch yourselves, or you also may be
tempted. Carry each other's burdens, and
in this way you will fulfill the law of Christ"
(NIV). You will need those who are spiritual
to help hold you up when you are seeking to
become free of unclean spirits.

The swine drowning brings this drama of Mark 5 to
a clear conclusion. All the issues at the root have collec-
tively drowned in the sea. As believers in Jesus we often
associate water with baptism. To be submerged in water
has always represented the process of dying to ourselves
and emerging again to a new life in Christ. The drowning
of the swine indicated that there would be no chance of
Legion being resurrected or experiencing new life. The
demons that kept gaining strength because no one could
deal with them had met their end. The drowning of the
pigs represented the end of the demons' reign of terror, the
end of their long season of torment. It represented the end
of their exploitation of the man and his community. There
is a finality in this moment in Mark chapter 5 verse 13 that
is purposeful and powerful.

The pigs drowning in the sea is almost reminiscent

of Pharaoh's army drowning in the Red Sea in Exodus 14. In both cases the drownings did not happen in isolation; they occurred publicly. In Exodus 14:13 Moses proclaimed God's promise to deal with the lingering torment of the Egyptians: "And Moses said to the people, 'Do not be afraid. Stand still, and see the salvation of the LORD, which He will accomplish for you today. For the Egyptians whom you see today, you shall see again no more forever.'"

After Pharaoh agreed to release the people of Israel from slavery in Egypt, he changed his mind and sent his army after them. The Israelites were hemmed in on every side with nowhere to go but across the Red Sea. You may know the story. God parted the sea so the Israelites could walk across on dry land. But Exodus 14:23 says, "And the Egyptians pursued and went after them into the midst of the sea, all Pharaoh's horses, his chariots, and his horsemen."

The Egyptians were determined to return the Israelites to bondage, but God had another plan. Exodus 14:27–28 says, "And Moses stretched out his hand over the sea; and when the morning appeared, the sea returned to its full depth, while the Egyptians were fleeing into it. So the LORD overthrew the Egyptians in the midst of the sea. Then the waters returned and covered the chariots, the horsemen, and all the army of Pharaoh that came into the sea after them. Not so much as one of them remained."

When God ends this chapter of demonic suppression in your life, it will be a public display of His power. God allows your character to be restored in the face of the same people before whom it was destroyed. The Lord always has a way of bringing you full circle so the miraculous healing power

He possesses will be witnessed by all who are looking to see how you will make it out of the situation.

Many people counted you out and believed the invasion of unclean spirits would be the end of you, but while those people were counting, they failed to count on the power of God, who cannot be defeated, to deliver you. Jesus the Deliverer will be sure to set you free right in the midst of the people who thought it was over for you so there will be no doubt that the transformation that has taken place in your life is authentic.

Those onlookers—gawkers, really—left you out in the tombs to die a public death; therefore the Lord will give you a public deliverance to make your oppressors aware that you are alive and free from the dead places, never to return to tomb living. The enemy oppressed you in public, and your oppressor must die in public. This is what Jesus did on the cross. As Paul wrote in Colossians 2:15, "And having spoiled principalities and powers, he made a shew of them openly, triumphing over them in it" (KJV).

Your willingness to invest in your deliverance—whether through time, tears, or treasure—will bring you into a season when you can finally experience the life God intended for you. Freedom is a gift from God, and now that you've gotten past this demonic nightmare, you are poised for a better and brighter future. John 8:36 promises that "if the Son makes you free, you shall be free indeed." When you come to this moment of freedom, you are going to have to believe it has happened.

German philosopher Friedrich Nietzsche once stated, "Freedom is the will to be responsible for ourselves."[3] To walk in freedom, you must take full responsibility for your life and no longer allow unclean spirits and forces of darkness to come in your life and take away your freedom. You were created to be a free moral agent. Living in a state that is any less than completely free is counter to God's purpose for you. Often when people have been victimized, there is a tendency to allow the residue of the trauma to linger long after the demon is gone. The children of Israel were delivered out of the oppression of Egypt, but it took a while for them to get Egypt out of them.

This is why I mentioned earlier that this is a process. Give yourself time to embrace this new season. Don't allow people or assignments to rush you. You've been through a lot, and rushing through your root work is neither healthy nor wise. God's desire is for you to walk in newness of life. In the medical field, when an incision is made, not only are stitches used to close the wound, but bandages are applied to protect it from infection and assist in the healing process.

Nobody experiences major surgery without going through recovery. Your recovery process may take a while, but you will get there. Allow prayer to be the bandage that covers your wound. When you pray, you can expect, as Paul wrote, that "the peace of God, which surpasses all understanding, will guard your hearts and minds through Christ Jesus" (Phil. 4:7).

ROOT WORK

1. Are you willing to make the sacrifice to live a life free of the tormenting spirits in your life? How much is your freedom worth to you?

2. What is your evacuation plan? How will you make unclean spirits leave your life?

3. Name the unclean spirits that are evident in the area in which you live. How do they impact your community?

4. What will be the impact of cleansing your community of the unclean spirits that continue cycles of systemic oppression?

5. After you are freed from the oppression of the unclean spirits, what measures will you put in place to remain free?

CHAPTER 10

Restoration:
The Rest of You Will Be the Best of You

THE MOST REWARDING thing about having an authentic encounter with Jesus is that He leaves you better than He found you. When you commit to the process of root work and get to the source of the struggle, you end up in a place of restoration. Though this journey was an arduous one for the man in the tombs, he experienced restoration at the root. After the legion was cast out of him and into the pigs that drowned, the Bible says in Mark 5:14–15, "So those who fed the swine fled, and they told it in the city and in the country. And they went out to see what it was that had happened. Then they came to Jesus, and saw the one who had been demon-possessed and had the legion, sitting and clothed and in his right mind. And they were afraid."

This man's witness gave anyone who had ever been attacked by the devil and his demonic forces hope. His mere presence was a testimony in itself because anyone who saw his state in the tombs knew he was basically a dead man walking. For the man to be sitting in the city from which he had been previously expelled, clothed and in his right mind, was a miracle. For an undetermined amount of time this man had been ostracized from his human characteristics. He had become wild and un-controllable, having taken on the traits of unclean spirits.

Yet his drastic transformation lets us know that although some deliverance may occur progressively, some forms of deliverance happen instantaneously. The man looked nothing like he had previously. His deliverance was such that Jesus immediately commissioned him to go share his testimony with his friends. This man was so full of joy about his newfound freedom that he not only shared his testimony among his friends, but the Scripture tells us that he also shared his message of the Lord's deliverance in Decapolis, which was a region of ten cities.

This man received complete deliverance instantly, and he did not try to hide what his life had been like before. He became a living testimony of the Lord's ability to heal and set us free. There is a life for you after your legion. God wants to heal you in the deep places of your life so you can experience true liberation. In other words, God's desire is that the rest of you becomes the best of you.

YOUR DELIVERANCE IS A BIG DEAL

The fact that the legion was cast out publicly made the incident of great interest to everyone in the community. The swineherds ran into the city and the country to tell what Jesus had done. Your deliverance is a big deal, and often the people whom you least expect will show interest in what God has done in your life. There are always people who need to see your transformation, especially those who had no faith for your deliverance. They need to see the power of God at work in your life.

The man who had been delivered initially wanted to go with Jesus, but Jesus told him to stay within the region instead. I can only assume that Jesus had the man stay in the area of his origin and of his oppression because he could serve as a greater witness to people who had seen him at his worst and now could see him at his best. If he would have traveled with Jesus, his story would not have had as much power, for people would have seen him only in his transformed state and would not appreciate how dramatically his life had been changed.

The people in his city and region needed to see him before and after because seeing what took place in his life would give them hope that the same thing could happen for them. People need to see you on the other side of your struggle. They need to see it so they can know it actually happened. They need to see it to strengthen their faith. Don't be alarmed or discouraged by the onlookers. God often uses what we have gone through to minister to others. Although there is an element in the crowd who might have a contrary agenda, God always gets the glory when you tell the story of what He has done.

It's incredibly important that the world sees some modern-day testimonies. Perhaps God is using this season in your life to show others His power. Some people may never read the Bible, but they will read the lives of those of us who proclaim its truth. It's one thing for people to hear about what God can do; it's another thing for them to see it for themselves. This man's deliverance drew a multitude of people. Often the same people who wrote you off and declared nothing could be done for you are the first ones God will put in your path when you are on the other side of your struggle. People in the city and in the country were informed about the man in the tombs. You may think others don't know, but they do. Just like the word of your immense struggle in the tombs spread, the word of your breakthrough will too.

When you have this moment, don't use it for self-promotion or to say, "I told y'all." Allow God to get all the glory. Walk in humility and gratitude for what God has done in your life. It's like the point Joseph came to in Genesis 50:20, when he said, "But as for you, ye thought evil against me; but God meant it unto good, to bring to pass, as it is this day, to save much people alive" (KJV). Joseph's story teaches us how to live out restoration without retaliation. Joseph's brothers sold him into slavery, and he endured lies and imprisonment before being elevated to second-in-command over Egypt, which put him in a position to save his brothers and their families. Joseph's story shows us that there is no need to get back at people for how they left you or how they wrote you off or how they spoke evil against you.

The people who worked against you were trying to bring about your demise, but their actions actually helped to push you forward into destiny. This is why the psalmist tells us, "Do not fret because of evildoers, nor be envious of the workers of iniquity. For they shall soon be cut down like the grass, and wither as the green herb" (Ps. 37:1–2). Those who do evil against you have term limits. The plan of devastation lodged against you will be truncated, and you will be brought into a season of restoration when Jesus brings social, emotional, and spiritual healing to your life.

STAGES OF RESTORATION

Restoration presents itself in different ways, but one thing is certain: when it occurs, it is apparent to the one who experiences it and those who witness it. Restoration can also be understood in stages. In the case of the man in Mark 5 the process of restoration occurred in the following stages:

Stage 1: Rest

After his deliverance the man was no longer running back and forth from the mountains to the tombs day and night. He also was in his right mind, which means he let go of the behavior of self-injury—crying out and cutting himself. According to the Mayo Clinic, "Nonsuicidal self-injury, often simply called self-injury, is the act of deliberately harming your own body, such as cutting or burning yourself. It's typically not meant as a suicide attempt. Rather, this type of self-injury is a harmful way to cope with emotional pain, intense anger and frustration."[1] After being delivered, the man found rest from his emotional pain. He was no longer cutting himself to cope with the inner turmoil he was experiencing.

Stage 2: Reconstruction

Every area in the man's life that had been destroyed was rebuilt. One significant area of reconstruction occurred in the man's social interaction. He was no longer an outcast, living on the margins of the city, vacillating from the mountains to the tombs. He was now mingling with others who came to see Jesus.

Stage 3: Restitution

Jesus sent the man back to his home and to his friends, which signifies the restitution that took place within his relationships. This man had been isolated from people far too long. Jesus knew he needed some time to reconnect with close, quality relationships and not merely build new relationships postdeliverance. He needed to be with people with whom he could be vulnerable and transparent about all he had been through. He needed authentic connections to ensure his restoration process was seen to completion.

In her book *Daring Greatly* research professor Brené Brown, PhD, wrote that she has learned the following about our need for connection: "Connection is why we're here; it is what gives purpose and meaning to our lives. The power that connection holds in our lives was confirmed when the main concern about connection emerged as the fear of disconnection; the fear that something we have done or failed to do, something about who we are or where we come from, has made us unlovable and unworthy of connection."[2]

This man did not need to become a spiritual superstar and go on tour with Jesus. He needed to go back home and be ministered to emotionally and socially as he continued to grow spiritually. Going back home also meant he was returning to a place of stability. People who face spiritual attack at the level this man experienced often suffer great loss, perhaps losing their jobs, their finances, or even their homes. When Jesus restores you, things that were lost will be replaced or recovered.

We get just a glimpse of what the restitution stage of the recovery process can look like in Joel 2:25–26: "And I will restore to you the years that the locust hath eaten, the cankerworm, and the caterpiller, and the palmerworm, my great army which I sent among you. And ye shall eat in plenty, and be satisfied, and praise the name of the LORD your God, that hath dealt wondrously with you: and my people shall never be ashamed" (KJV). In the restitution stage God brings back the things you lost and returns you to where you were before the legion took control of your life.

Stage 4: Reset

Instead of the being the one who had things published about him throughout the city, the man became the one who delivered the news as he told of all Jesus had done for him. His witness caused others to marvel at the power of God evident in his life. Restoration includes a hard reset of your life and allows you to be transformed spiritually. You will no longer be in a dead place that was governed by forces of darkness. When the Lord resets your life, you will walk in the light, and others will see the light within you and stand in awe of God's glory.

PROOF OF NEW LIFE

When you are restored at the root, there is verifiable proof. For the man who was in the tombs, the first thing people noticed was that he was sitting. On the surface that may sound like an insignificant thing to point out, but it reveals a powerful aspect of his restoration. The man had been living among the tombs for a lengthy period of time. The trauma he experienced caused him to go frequently between the mountain and the tombs. Day and night he cried out, going up and down. It must have been exhausting, which is why his sitting down is so significant.

The objective of unclean spirits is to wear you down so you have no strength to fight. They want to wear you down so you have no strength to fulfill your God-given purpose. Sitting represents rest. It represents an opportunity for recovery. It represents a season for reflection, for you to regroup and come back stronger. In this time of restoration God is giving you an opportunity to finally rest and recuperate from what you have experienced. You can't experience restoration without rest. You can't even spell *restoration* without *rest*.

So often we find ourselves coming out of a season of trauma and running to the next thing. God wants you to be still for a moment and allow Him to restore you. You can't run to another relationship right after you've come out of a bad one. So many people run from one thing to the next, which prevents them from fully experiencing restoration. Allow the Lord to do what Psalm 23:2–3 promises: "He makes me to lie down in green pastures; He leads me beside the still waters. He restores my soul."

This cessation from any activity is not a sign of laziness; rather, it is an opportunity for God to restore the deep places in your life. The apostle Paul sat three years with the Jews after his conversion experience before embarking upon his new ministry. After years of persecuting

Christians, Paul gave himself time to reset and prepare for his new assignment of preaching Christ.

You may go through a season when you can't get the next job you want or get in the program you desire. You have to trust God's plan for your life and know that He is providentially at work creating time for you to get stronger and better. Rather than be discouraged at the opportunities you didn't get, you should rejoice because greater ones are in your future. Use this "sitting" season wisely and allow God to do what only He can do for you. You've been through so much, and you deserve this moment. This is about your next season. This is about your being healthy physically, emotionally, and spiritually. I encourage you to sit until God says move. Sit there without feeling obligated by someone else's expectations. Sit there until God completes His work in your life. After all the things you've endured, you deserve this seat.

The next thing Mark 5:15 says is that he was clothed. The fact that it was obvious he was clothed suggests that the unclean spirits had stripped him of his garments. The Scriptures often mention people being stripped of their garments. We see this when Paul and Silas were persecuted after casting out the demon from the young girl. The Bible says in Acts 16:22, "Then the multitude rose up together against them; and the magistrates tore off their clothes and commanded them to be beaten with rods." We see this in the Passion account when Jesus was stripped and beaten before His crucifixion. We also see it in the story of the prodigal son; when he was at his lowest point, he was in the pigpen stripped of his clothing. This is why his father put a robe on him upon his return home.

When someone is stripped of his clothing, it is an attempt to publicly humiliate and bring shame. This is what demons want to do. Whether physically or spiritually, being unclothed represents being exposed. This man experienced exposure on so many levels. The enemy rejoices in exposing you in your weakness so he can gloat in his power. God's desire is for you to be clothed. After the man was set free, he was clothed. The passage never says how or who clothed him, but when we see him restored, he is sitting and covered.

Maybe you are reading this and you feel like what you've gone through has left you exposed. When God restores you at the root, He takes interest in your covering. It doesn't matter how Satan has exposed and exploited you, God will clothe you with new garments so you can move forward in newness of life. He will do as the psalmist declared:

> Whoever dwells in the shelter of the Most High will rest in the shadow of the Almighty. I will say of the Lord, "He is my refuge and my fortress, my God, in whom I trust." Surely he will save you from the fowler's snare and from the deadly pestilence. He will cover you with his feathers, and under his wings you will find refuge; his faithfulness will be your shield and rampart. You will not fear the terror of night, nor the arrow that flies by day, nor the pestilence that stalks in the darkness, nor the plague that destroys at midday. A thousand may fall at your

side, ten thousand at your right hand, but it will not
come near you.

—PSALM 91:1–7, NIV

Please know that you aren't the only person who has
experienced this. I'm reminded daily that everything I
do for the Lord I do because He has me covered. It's not
because I'm so good; rather, it's because He's so good. He
loves us so much that He will not allow exposure and
shame to define our destiny. He restores at the root by
covering us in every place the enemy attempted to expose.

The final confirmation of restoration is perhaps the most
important. The Bible says the man who had been living
among the tombs was in his right mind. If there is one area
that confirms without a doubt that you've been restored at
the root, it is this. The demonic assaults that occur in all of
our lives have a tremendous impact on our minds. Although
so much of the story in Mark 5 focuses on the external
effects of his ordeal, we can't lose sight of the internal mental
torment he experienced as well. As I mentioned previously,
when Satan pulls us into isolation, he begins the interrogation. Considering what you've had to endure, being in your
right mind is nothing short of a miracle.

There have been times in my life, and I'm sure in yours
as well, when I could feel the weight of the struggle
impacting my mind. This is why the Bible gives us the
following instructions in Hebrews 12:1–2: "Therefore we
also, since we are surrounded by so great a cloud of wit-
nesses, let us lay aside every weight, and the sin which so
easily ensnares us, and let us run with endurance the race

that is set before us, *looking unto Jesus, the author and finisher of our faith*, who for the joy that was set before Him endured the cross, despising the shame, and has sat down at the right hand of the throne of God" (emphasis added).

Satan wants to disrupt your life and cause you to be mentally distraught and distracted, but Jesus is here to keep you focused. All Jesus needs you to do is look to Him. When you are distraught, you convince yourself that your situation is beyond recovery or that you will never come out of it. You feel like the psalmist, crying out, "Why are you cast down, O my soul? And why are you disquieted within me?" (Ps. 42:5).

When you are in this place of hopelessness, it's difficult to share what you are experiencing because you don't want to be seen as a quitter. All of us have had these moments, and it is not uncommon among those who experience spiritual warfare. I remember going through a spiritual attack that had convinced me it would never let up. I cried out to God many nights, pleading for Him to make it stop. The more I pleaded, the worse it became. My mind was under attack, and I couldn't see a path forward.

I was distracted, which is the other side of the mental attack. When your focus is on what you are going through, you lose sight of what you are going to. When you are in the midst of the attack, you often are so consumed with the chaos that you are unable to focus on the task before you. This is why so many people don't finish projects and complete assignments. I've been in acute situations and what should have been minor began to look major because

I lost focus. This is why you have to step back and allow God to refine your perspective.

The mental attacks you experienced were real, so it's important that you allow yourself time to regroup and refocus. Psychological research teaches us that "recovering from a traumatic experience requires that the painful emotions be thoroughly processed. Trauma feelings cannot be repressed or forgotten. If they are not dealt with directly, the distressing feelings and troubling events replay over and over in the course of a lifetime, creating a condition known as post-traumatic stress disorder."[3] Going through a traumatic experience doesn't mean you cannot go back to a normal life, but you must take time to work through what you went through so you can operate at 100 percent.

Although this man experienced a systematic attack upon his life that should have left him with some permanent mental challenges, God kept him through it all. I've often said that we thank God for a variety of things, as we should. We thank Him for the house, car, job, and family, among many other things. When you've gone through the level of attack you have and know where your mind was and could have been today, you are just grateful that God kept you! You came out of an insane situation still sane.

It doesn't mean anything if you come out of a traumatic situation but your mind is not right. Mental health is just as important as physical health. The man who dwelt among the tombs no longer cut himself and was able to finally rest from the exhaustion his ordeal created, but being in his right mind suggests that he was in a place of wholeness and peace. God wants to bring you to this place. It is His desire that you are no longer tormented by the memories of your past. When you are restored at the root, there is no residue of what occurred in your life. Your future is not crippled by your past. You truly are in a good place where God can download new vision into your life.

God has some amazing things planned for your life. It is a fact that what did not kill you only made you stronger. Your next season is going to be so phenomenal. You are a survivor. You've survived what some thought you never would. What you learned through the experience will be valuable where God is taking you. Regardless of the demonic assaults we encounter in life, God always has a way of reminding us that He controls the outcome. I tell people all the time that if God allowed it, it's going to bless you. It may be hard to see the blessing while you are in it, but it appears on the other side. David's word in Psalm 30:5 is so true: "Weeping may endure for a night, but joy comes in the morning." When you are restored at the root, you no longer empower your past pain and allow it to influence your present and future. You can declare today that you are truly over it. You are restored at the root!

ROOT WORK

1. What areas in your life are in need of true liberation that comes from God? In answering this question, consider the following: Do you feel fulfilled in life? Do you believe you are walking in your purpose? Are you optimistic about the future? Answering these questions can help you determine the areas of your life that need to experience God's liberating power so you can move forward.

2. How have the challenges you have faced helped to shape your testimony? How have you been made stronger by what you have endured?

3. If you have received deliverance from demonic attack, where are you in the restoration process? What stage are you in?

4. After you have been healed, God calls you to help others, not hurt them. What steps will you take to witness to others after you are fully delivered and made whole?

5. If you recently overcame a spiritual attack, have you taken time to heal physically, emotionally, socially, and spiritually? If the answer is yes, list at least one specific area in which you have received healing, and explain how you arrived at that place of healing. If the answer is no, what is keeping you from moving to a place of healing physically, emotionally, socially, and spiritually?

Conclusion

I PRAY THAT BY now you've been challenged to look at your life and others' lives beyond the surface. The struggles you face have a source, and you now have the tools to discover it. You have been equipped to dig down to the root of your issues so you can experience freedom and restoration. No matter how much pain you have endured, no matter how many times the devil has tried to take you out, God is in control of your future. Never give up on yourself or others because God always has the power to deliver.

The story of the man in the tombs touches us on numerous levels because it gives us a new way to view the multifaceted challenges we experience in life. You don't necessarily have to do anything wrong to encounter struggles in life, but you do have to understand the necessity of root work to overcome them.

I've gone through life with many private struggles and had no idea of their origin. I know firsthand how easy it is to keep showing up and masking inner issues with public ministry. It appeared safer that way. What I discovered is that this could continue for only so long. Legion

187

is exhausting. Carrying around so many underlying and unreconciled issues only corrodes us at the core. I've enjoyed so many amazing positions and platforms that some would dream to have, yet I realized that my potential was being truncated as long as I avoided the root work.

As I mentioned previously, doing root work is not easy, but it's necessary if you want to live in truth. I've made so many mistakes in life. Some could have cost me everything, but the grace of God gave me an extension. I believe this book is a part of that extension so others will know the value of being restored at the root. Image means nothing if there is no integrity. We all must mature to a place where we realize what matters most in life. I didn't want to tarnish the kingdom of God by allowing the legion to exploit my life for even one more day.

So I allowed God in to do the work of shining His light on the areas that were not in alignment with His Spirit. After the unclean areas were identified, I had to make a conscious decision to be delivered from what was seeking to damage me. I had to make a choice to either confront the unclean spirits or let them continue to suppress my life, which would have led only to internal conflict. I made the choice to conquer the unclean spirits in my life by allowing the Lord to set me free and remain free. I am able to stay free by remaining connected to God through praying and studying the Word of God daily and by having partners in place to help me to continue to walk in my deliverance. Ultimately I had to make the decision to leave a situation of pain and bondage to live a life of peace and freedom. I did this by surrendering to the power of God. I encourage you to do the same. Because I went to the root, I have been restored.

No matter what you have gone through or might be currently dealing with, I pray you find comfort in knowing what's possible. Jesus said in Matthew 19:26 that "with God all things are possible," even those things that are impossible by human standards. It is God's desire that you come through your struggles whole. You have an amazing future ahead of you, and God will use this experience, although challenging, as a catalyst for you to impact others. Your trauma will be transformational.

After the man was restored at the root, Jesus commanded him, "Go home to your friends, and tell them what great things the Lord has done for you, and how He has had compassion on you" (Mark 5:19). Jesus sent him home because what he experienced had separated him from his community. Your restoration will include being reunited with friends and family. This man, like you and me, had a new narrative. Being restored at the root changes us, and we must go back and share what has transpired in our lives so others can find encouragement.

I fly often, and on one flight I found myself sitting next to a pilot. As we were going through the Santa Ana winds, we began to experience some intense turbulence. I am a frequent flier, but the level of turbulence we felt was a cause for concern. Before anyone could get too nervous, the pilot announced that it would last for only fifteen minutes. I was curious how he knew that considering we were going through that area for the first time. I inquired of the pilot sitting next to me, and what he told me was life-changing. He said pilots are required by the FAA to report weather conditions to the tower so the information can be shared with other planes in the area. He said planes ahead of us were sending back data so the planes behind them would know what to expect.

God is allowing you to go through this so you can be restored at the root; then those behind you will know that trouble doesn't last always, and if God brought you through it, He is able to bring them through as well. We never go through just for us. Our tests are transformed into testimonies that encourage others. You never know how your testimony will bless another person. There are people who are on edge. Many are in a place of deep contemplation about what to do next. For some, their options are running out, but your story will reignite their hope in what's possible. Your very presence will speak to the power of God to restore.

Allow the Holy Spirit to do a work in you. He is greater than any force that has invaded your life. He is able to heal the broken places and close up the wounds of your past. He is there to fill every void and to comfort you through the recovery process. Allow the Holy Spirit to have full control in your life. He will lead you and teach you as you move into a new season. The Holy Spirit also will give you courage to rise up from the ashes of your situation and reconnect to the community where God sends you because the tormenting spirit will be gone.

A community is a powerful thing. It is like a beautiful quilt made from a variety of interwoven stories and experiences. That is what makes it amazing. If those stories are not given space to exist, we rob ourselves of the beauty in the community. The family, church, and community at large must welcome with open arms those who have been restored. They must be reminded that they are still family. They must experience what the prodigal son experienced upon his return home—a celebration of the fact that those who were bound are now set free.

When God has restored you at the root, don't distance yourself from the power of community. Go home! Don't live in shame concerning your past. You have overcome what some thought you never would. Your family needs what you have. Your faith community needs what you have. Your physical community needs what you have. So many people are struggling and don't know why. You do. You understand firsthand the process of getting to the root. God trusted you with trouble because He knew you would give Him the glory when you came out. Use what you've gone through in a way that glorifies God and edifies His people.

You've been through some painful chapters, but your story is still being written. Let God restore you at the root and begin a new chapter of greatness. Let Him create your future with healthy roots to produce godly fruit.

Notes

INTRODUCTION

1. Ryan LeStrange, *Overcoming Spiritual Attack: Identify and Break Eight Common Symptoms* (Lake Mary, FL: Charisma House, 2016), 9.

CHAPTER 1

1. C. S. Lewis, *The Chronicles of Narnia* (New York: HarperCollins, 1956), 713.
2. Cindy Trimm, *The Rules of Engagement: The Art of Strategic Prayer and Spiritual Warfare* (Lake Mary, FL: Charisma House, 2008), 50.
3. Blue Letter Bible, s.v. *"tohuw,"* accessed April 3, 2019, https://www.blueletterbible.org/lang/Lexicon/Lexicon.cfm?strongs=H8414&t=kjv; Blue Letter Bible, s.v. *"bohuw,"* accessed April 3, 2019, https://www.blueletterbible.org/lang/Lexicon/Lexicon.cfm?strongs=H922&t=kjv.
4. Blue Letter Bible, s.v. *"bamah,"* accessed May 13, 2019, https://www.blueletterbible.org/lang/lexicon/lexicon.cfm?page=1&strongs=H1116&t=KJV.

CHAPTER 2

1. Frank T. McAndrew, "The Perils of Social Isolation," *Psychology Today*, November 12, 2016, https://www.psychologytoday.com/us/blog/out-the-ooze/201611/the-perils-social-isolation.
2. Monte Burke, "Loneliness Can Kill You," *Forbes*, August 6, 2009, https://www.forbes.com/forbes/2009/0824/opinions-neuroscience-loneliness-ideas-opinions.html#1ccc69fe7f85.
3. Burke, "Loneliness Can Kill You."

CHAPTER 3

1. Gretchen Gavett, "A Rare Look at the Police Tactics That Can Lead to False Confessions," *Frontline*, December 9, 2011, https://www.pbs.org/wgbh/frontline/article/a-rare-look-at-the-police-tactics-that-can-lead-to-false-confessions/.
2. Melissa Bienvenu, "Are You a High-Functioning Alcoholic?," WebMD, May 30, 2017, https://www.webmd.com/mental-health/addiction/features/high-functioning-alcoholic#1.

CHAPTER 4

1. Frank and Ida Mae Hammond, *Pigs in the Parlor: The Practical Guide to Deliverance* (Kirkwood, WA: Impact Christian Books, 2010), 51.
2. Kimberly Daniels, *Clean House—Strong House* (Lake Mary, FL: Charisma House, 2003), 17, italics in the original.

3. Michelle Alexander, *The New Jim Crow: Mass Incarceration in the Age of Colorblindness* (New York: The New Press, 2012), 18.

CHAPTER 5

1. Catherine Antoine, "Seniors Use Prayer to Cope With Stress; Prayer No. 1 Alternative Remedy," University of Florida, December 28, 2000, http://news.ufl.edu/ archive/2000/12/seniors-use-prayer-to-cope-with-stress-prayer-no-1-alternative-remedy.html.
2. Stephen A. Diamond, "Anger Disorder (Part Two): Can Bitterness Become a Mental Disorder?," *Psychology Today*, June 3, 2009, https://www.psychologytoday.com/ us/blog/evil-deeds/200906/anger-disorder-part-two-can-bitterness-become-mental-disorder.
3. Friedrich Nietzsche, *Ecce Homo*, trans. Anthony M. Ludovici (London: T. N. Foulis, 1911), 21, https://www. gutenberg.org/files/52190/52190-h/52190-h.htm.
4. Richard J. Krejcir, "Statistics on Pastors: 2016 Update," Institute of Church Leadership Development, accessed April 1, 2019, http://www.churchleadership.org/apps/ articles/default.asp?blogid=4545&view=post&articleid =Statistics-on-Pastors-2016-Update&link=1&fldKeywo rds=&fldAuthor=&fldTopic=0.
5. Sarah Eekhoff Zylstra, "Why Pastors Are Committing Suicide," The Gospel Coalition, November 23, 2016, https://www.thegospelcoalition.org/article/why-pastors-are-committing-suicide/; *Study of Acute Mental Illness and Christian Faith*, Research Report, LifeWay Research, 2014, 18, http://lifewayresearch. com/wp-content/uploads/2014/09/Acute-Mental-Illness-and-Christian-Faith-Research-Report-1.pdf.

6. Zylstra, "Why Pastors Are Committing Suicide."

CHAPTER 6

1. Plato, *Charmides, or Temperance*, trans. Benjamin Jowett, accessed April 3, 2019, http://classics.mit.edu/Plato/charmides.html.
2. Jim Patterson, "Worship Is Good for Your Health: Vanderbilt Study," May 31, 2017, Vanderbilt University, https://news.vanderbilt.edu/2017/05/31/worship-is-good-for-your-health-vanderbilt-study/.
3. Shahram Heshmat, "Basics of Identity," *Psychology Today*, December 8, 2014, https://www.psychologytoday.com/us/blog/science-choice/201412/basics-identity.
4. Heshmat, "Basics of Identity."
5. Quote by Oprah Winfrey adapted from statement by Maya Angelou. See "When People Show You Who They Are, Believe Them," Oprah's Life Class, October 26, 2011, http://www.oprah.com/oprahs-lifeclass/when-people-show-you-who-they-are-believe-them-video#ixzz5hJDq2VA9.

CHAPTER 7

1. Daniels, *Clean House—Strong House*, 29–30.
2. Lewis Howes, "10 Lessons for Entrepreneurs From Coach John Wooden," *Forbes*, October 19, 2012, https://www.forbes.com/sites/lewishowes/2012/10/19/10-lessons-for-entrepreneurs-from-coach-john-wooden/#598cb67316d5.

CHAPTER 8

1. "What Is Excavation?," Ohio State Archaeological Excavations in Greece, The Ohio State University,

accessed April 3, 2019, https://greekarchaeology.osu. edu/arch-edu/excavation.

2. "What Is Excavation?," The Ohio State University.

3. "What Is Excavation?," The Ohio State University.

4. Blue Letter Bible, s.v. "*legiōn*," accessed April 3, 2019, https://www.blueletterbible.org/lang/Lexicon/Lexicon. cfm?strongs=G3003&t=kjv.

5. Pamela Paul, "With God as My Shrink," *Psychology Today*, June 9, 2016, https://www.psychologytoday.com/ us/articles/200505/god-my-shrink.

6. "13 Stats on Mental Health and the Church," Facts & Trends, May 1, 2018, https://factsandtrends. net/2018/05/01/13-stats-on-mental-health-and-the-church/.

CHAPTER 9

1. Lauren Camera, "In Most States, Poorest School Districts Get Less Funding," *U.S. News & World Report*, February 27, 2018, https://www.usnews.com/ news/best-states/articles/2018-02-27/in-most-states-poorest-school-districts-get-less-funding; see also Ivy Morgan and Ary Amerikaner, "Funding Gaps 2018," The Education Trust, accessed April 9, 2019, https://edtrust.org/wp-content/uploads/2014/09/ FundingGapReport_2018_FINAL.pdf.

2. Trimm, *The Rules of Engagement*, 51–52.

3. Friedrich Nietzsche, *Twilight of the Idols With the Antichrist and Ecce Homo* (Ware, Hertfordshire: Wordsworth Editions Limited, 2007), sec. 38.

CHAPTER 10

1. Mayo Clinic, "Self-Injury/Cutting," Mayo Foundation for Medical Education and Research (MFMER), accessed April 4, 2019, https://www.mayoclinic.org/diseases-conditions/self-injury/symptoms-causes/syc-20350950.

2. Brené Brown, *Daring Greatly: How the Courage to Be Vulnerable Transforms the Way We Live, Love, Parent, and Lead* (New York: Avery, 2012), 253.

3. Ellen McGrath, "Recovering From Trauma," *Psychology Today*, June 9, 2016, https://www.psychologytoday.com/us/articles/200111/recovering-trauma.

ACKNOWLEDGMENTS

THIS BOOK WOULD not be possible without the support of so many who prayed for me throughout the process of writing it. First and foremost, my beloved wife, Dr. Stephaine Walker—your willingness to give me space and grace to spend countless hours hearing from God while putting pen to paper is beyond appreciated. You are truly my Superwoman. Your prayers and support continue to sustain me and remind me daily how much God loves me to have given you to me.

To my beautiful two children, Jovanni and Joseph the Fourth—you guys keep my feet on the ground. No matter what the world sees in me, you see Dad. I pray daily that I inspire you to reach for everything God has for your life and to never settle.

I'm thankful for my parents, Rosa and Joseph Walker. You have been my inspiration, and I stand on your shoulders. You believed in me and saw in me what I didn't see in myself. You continued to push me to believe in what God has deposited within me. I am a blessed son.

To the greatest church on the planet, I say thanks. Mount Zion church has been the place where God has allowed me to serve. To lead a people who support vision and the visionary is humbling. I'm so thankful for your support and the unwavering prayers you guys send up on my behalf.

Thank you to the Full Gospel Baptist Church Fellowship International for continuing to undergird what God does in my life. I'm thankful to lead such a powerful and significant reformation that impacts the world in such a profound way.

Last but not least, I'm so thankful to God for His grace and mercy. Root work is challenging and cannot be accomplished apart from a relationship with Jesus Christ. I give God all the praise for the anointing to write this work, and I pray that God's people are edified and God is glorified.

ABOUT THE AUTHOR

Bishop Joseph Warren Walker III is the senior pastor of the historic Mount Zion Baptist Church of Nashville, Tennessee. Born in Shreveport, Louisiana, to Deacon Joseph and Mrs. Rosa Walker, Bishop Walker received a bachelor of arts degree from Southern University, a master of divinity from Vanderbilt University, and a doctor of ministry from Princeton Theological Seminary. He holds two honorary doctorates from Meharry Medical College and Southern University and currently serves on the Meharry Medical College board of trustees and the Citizens Savings Bank board of directors. In October 2016 he was appointed by Tennessee governor Bill Haslam to serve on the Tennessee State University board of trustees, of which he is the chairman. Bishop Walker currently serves as the international presiding bishop in the Full Gospel Baptist Church Fellowship International, a position he has held since July 2013, when he was chosen to succeed founding international presiding bishop Paul S. Morton Sr.

In 1992, at the age of twenty-four, Bishop Walker began his pastorate at Mount Zion with 175 members. Presently the ministry has grown to over thirty thousand and continues to grow at a phenomenal rate of over two thousand souls per year. Under Bishop Walker's leadership Mount Zion has expanded beyond its original location on historic Jefferson Street to eight weekly services in three physical locations. It also ministers to millions around the world through its virtual church (www.mtzionanywhere.tv).

A prolific writer, "Bishop," as he is fondly called, is the author of thirteen books, including one written with his wife, Dr. Stephaine H. Walker, titled Becoming a Couple of Destiny, and No Opportunity Wasted: The Art of Execution (NOW). Whether you are in the ivory halls of the academy, corporate boardrooms, or even the hallowed pews of our places of worship, NOW inundates you with practical strategies about how to execute vision. Your vision means nothing if it is dormant in some theoretical space but never comes down to the real world of practicality and implementation.

His inspiring messages make him a sought-after university commencement speaker. Bishop Walker is a regular guest on the Rickey Smiley Morning Show and has been a guest on CNN, MSNBC, and The Roland Martin Show. His wife, Dr. Stephaine H. Walker, is a former assistant professor of pediatrics and neonatology at Vanderbilt University. Both agree that their most joyous accomplishments to date have been the births of their daughter, Jovanni Willow, in May 2012, and their son, Joseph Warren Walker IV, in February 2018.

DON'T TREAT THE CONSEQUENCE.
TREAT THE CAUSE.

I am so happy you read my book. I hope you have gained a **greater understanding** of the issues that are consuming your life and have been guided toward living a life of **social**, **emotional**, and **spiritual wellness**.

As My Way of Saying Thank You…
I AM OFFERING YOU A COUPLE OF GIFTS:

- E-book: *Restored at the Root*
- E-book: *Everlasting Hope* published by Charisma House

To get these **FREE GIFTS**, please go to:
www.RestoredAtTheRoot.com/gift

Thanks again and God bless you,
Bishop Joseph W. Walker III

CHARISMA
HOUSE

16403